MY FIRST PLAY

An Anthology of Theatrical Beginnings

Compiled by Nick Hern

1988–2013

NICK HERN BOOKS
London
www.nickhernbooks.co.uk

A Nick Hern Book

My First Play
first published in Great Britain in 2013
by Nick Hern Books Limited, The Glasshouse,
49a Goldhawk Road, London W12 8QP

Designed and typeset by Nick Hern Books, London
Printed and bound by CPI Group (UK) Ltd, Croydon, CR0 4YY

A CIP catalogue record for this book is available from the
British Library

ISBN 978 1 84842 339 8

My First Play

Contents

CONTENTS

Introduction

In 2013, the year I'm writing this, the publishing firm I set up in 1988 celebrated its twenty-fifth anniversary. As a publisher I naturally wanted to publish something special to mark the occasion. Rejecting the idea of a 'Reader' consisting of bleeding chunks of plays and books by the various authors on the Nick Hern Books list, I hit instead on the idea of asking pretty well everyone whose plays or books had been regularly published by NHB to write a little piece on 'My First Play'.

I explained to them that this could be 'the first play you ever saw, the first play you wrote/acted in/directed, the first one that blew your socks off, the play that made you want to go into the theatre etc., etc.' And I attached a piece I had just written on the subject by way of proving to myself it could be done – and that it could be fun.

The result was instantaneous. Pieces started coming in that very evening. The first was by Caryl Churchill with a note that read: 'This is the sort of thing that if I don't do it at once the time will rush by and I won't do it at all.' Then a piece by Ella Hickson, full of the joy of a fascinating discovery. Then Larry Kramer, Stephen Jeffreys and Alexi Kaye Campbell all came through within a day or two. After the trickle came a gratifying flood, the results of which fill this book.

People who were absurdly busy were often the most punctilious – Bruce Norris and Dominic Cooke both sent pieces while opening *The Low Road* at the Royal Court, Richard Eyre from Chichester where he was opening *The Pajama Game*, Howard Brenton from Hampstead where he was arresting Ai Weiwei, Joanna Murray-Smith from the opening of her new play at the Sydney Theatre Company, Oliver Ford Davies from the exhaustion of an extended tour of *Goodnight Mister Tom*, and Polly Teale from mid-rehearsals for Alexi's *Bracken Moor*. Tanya Ronder struggled out from under the *Table* at the National to deliver her piece, while Conor McPherson managed his while attending to the revival of one play, *The Weir*, and the premiere of another, *The Night Alive*, both at the Donmar. It wasn't all theatre, though: Elaine Murphy, six months pregnant, overcame 'baby brain' to write a piece, while Chloë Moss delivered hers soon after giving birth. And these are just the stories I heard about. *Everyone* whose pieces appear here generously put aside pressing obligations to make their contributions, for which I'm humbly grateful.

And what heart-warming, revelatory, hilarious and touching pieces they are – all in all a marvellous birthday present to NHB. I read many of them with eyes misting over at the joyous – yet complex – innocence on display. And it occurred to me that each of them in their way is the story of a love affair...

So, to get the ball rolling, here's mine.

Nick Hern

The first play I ever acted in was *As You Like It* – playing Silvius, the lovelorn shepherd. I was eleven and at an all-boys prep school. Daniels minor was my Phoebe. The first play I starred in was *The Taming of the Shrew* in my last year at school. My seventeen-year-old Petruchio wooed a Kate played by Nick Sherwin, brother of David, the future author of *If...*, which was self-confessedly based on the school we all attended. Which, say people who've seen the film, explains a lot about me... My servant, Grumio, was played by Timothy (James Bond) Dalton.

The first play I fell in love with on the page was Harold Pinter's *The Dumb Waiter*, also in my last year at school. After a diet of compulsory Shakespeare, Racine and Schiller in the way of drama (I was doing French and German at A level), I was set alight by the raw street-cred of Pinter's dialogue and the alluring mysteriousness of his characters – who *were* these magnetically attractive people, opening the doors of perception for a sheltered public-schoolboy? When I joined Methuen as their drama editor in 1974, I became Pinter's publisher, and it took me two years or more to stop pinching myself as I sipped Chablis in his study going over proofs of the latest masterpiece. Back in 1961, my discovery of Pinter had led me on to all those Angry Young Playwrights being collected and published in the newly launched Penguin New English Dramatists, the fourteen volumes of which are still on my shelves. And so I added Wesker, Osborne, Arden to my acquaintance as well as N.F. Simpson, Peter Shaffer, John Whiting and Bernard Kops. When my school sanctioned a rare sixth-form

3

outing to London, I made a bee-line for the fabled Royal Court, determined to see whatever was on. I struck lucky: John Dexter's charismatic premiere production of *Chips with Everything*, with its brilliantly choreographed silent raid on the coke-store – my first lesson in how drama doesn't necessarily need dialogue to engage an audience and score a point.

The first play I ever published was one that Methuen had already committed to, so not my choice. *The Incredible Vanishing!!!!* (four exclamation marks), which was Denise Coffey's take on Christina Rossetti's *Goblin Market*, had just been staged at the Young Vic under Frank Dunlop's regime. It was an attractive and energetic play for children, and Denise was a helpfully attractive and energetic author to work with on my first publication. I no longer have a copy, but I see it's available via Amazon for the customary penny. The first play I *chose* to publish was *Hitting Town*, Stephen Poliakoff's 'breakthrough' at the ripe old age of twenty-two. At that time Methuen was still publishing all its plays in both hardback and paperback, and publishing them some months after the premiere. Coming from teaching in the provinces where we needed *immediate* access to the plays that London was seeing, I was determined to short-circuit this cumbersome publication procedure. The result was that Stephen's play and many by subsequent up-and-coming writers were published in hideous KwikFit editions, with the text set in double columns and the covers printed in black only. They were pretty universally disliked, but they served their turn by greatly reducing the interval between the appearance of the play on stage and its appearance in print.

I struck lucky again with the first play I published when I set up Nick Hern Books in 1988. Nicholas Wright's *Mrs Klein*, now – like Nick Hern Books itself – twenty-five years old, has become a modern classic. So proud was I of this first product of my new imprint that I blazoned 'A NICK HERN BOOK' all over the front cover. 'Humph!' said the author on seeing the first copies, 'Your name appears rather more times than mine.' The banner headline was promptly dropped.

The first play I ever saw in the theatre was, I'm pretty sure, something called *The Silver Curlew* by (I've just looked this up) Eleanor Farjeon. I was six, and, my mother being ill, it fell to my father to entertain me that Christmas. Off we went to a matinee at the cavernous Kentish Town Forum. My memory is that there were only about six other people in the audience, and we were moved forward from the cheap seats at the back. I found the proceedings on stage tedious and fey, an opinion I'm sure I would still share with my younger self. The cliché about falling in love with the theatre at first sight failed miserably in my case, and my father's well-meaning experiment was not repeated. Instead, as with real-life love affairs, I had to make my own choices, and, as in real life, theatrical love exploded when least expected. The Christmas 1960 school holidays saw me take over operating a follow-spot for the pantomime at the New Theatre, Bromley (now the Churchill). A more enterprising older friend had sweet-talked his way into this job but had to absent himself for a couple of days to attend a round of Oxbridge interviews. I shadowed him for one performance, and then I was on my own. The anxiety, the thrill, above all the *glamour* – I can still recapture that heady brew today. And, despite the thousands of plays I've watched, read and published since, I have to admit that training my follow-spot onto the principal boy that Christmas over fifty years ago as she sang 'Moon River' to the principal girl was the moment I fell irretrievably in love with theatre.

In italics at the foot of each piece is a listing of that author's plays and/or books published by NHB. The dates given are of first publication as a Nick Hern Book.

Mike Alfreds

As a child, I wanted to act. Rotting in some attic – or so I fervently pray – is a technicolour home movie of me, aged six, impersonating Carmen Miranda, with a turban of real fruit and a towel, and multicoloured plastic rings, the sort for identifying chickens, dangling from my ears. My First Stage Appearance – or half appearance – was as the third of a trio of bluebells in a school pantomime. We wore gauzy blue costumes with floppy hats. Due to the incompetence of the first bluebell, I barely got out of the wings. My First Speaking Role was in the following year's school play, when I was promoted to the role of Amundsen, of whom I'd never heard, and had one line: 'My name is Amundsen and I'm going to get to the South Pole before anyone else.' Then, bearing the Norwegian flag, I had to run in a circle faster than the boy playing Scott who was running around in the opposite direction with the Union Jack. At grammar school, I played Madam Wang, mother of the eponymous heroine, *Lady Precious Stream*, and had to learn to mince like an ancient dowager with bound feet. Not easy; I was an awkward child, large for my age. The Big Time came when I got to play the heroine rather than her mother: Raina, in Shaw's *Arms and the Man*. I dread to think… Then my voice broke – and nobody wanted me.

As a child, I wanted to write plays. My First Play started: 'Act One, Scene One. The living room of a charming country house. There is a sofa filled with bright cushions downstage centre and a cocktail cabinet stage left. Below that, a door leads to the dining room. A door stage right leads to the hall. Up centre, French windows open onto a lawn and flower beds in full bloom. The French windows are open'. Nobody ever came through those windows. That was as far as I got. The First Play I ever read (apart from those above) had been *Hay Fever*.

As a child, I went to the theatre a lot. The First Professional Play I saw was at a matinee at the Criterion in Piccadilly Circus. It was *The Guinea Pig* by a playwright called Warren Chetham Strode about a grammar-school boy who won a scholarship to a public school. It wakened me to the iniquities of class.

As a teenager, The First Play that gave me some insight into what Great Acting really might be was Clifford Odets's *The Country Girl*, here called *Winter Journey* (Heaven forbid it should be confused with our very own *Country Wife*) at the long-gone St James's Theatre. In it, Michael Redgrave and Sam Wanamaker seemed to be improvising recklessly – dangerously. I got very excited.

The First Play that showed me that comedy and tragedy could be contained in one and the same moment was the Oliviers' playing of the Screen Scene in *The School for Scandal* at the then New Theatre, now the Noël Coward. This revelation was raised to dizzying heights many years later by Jacques Charon and Robert Hirsch in the Comédie-Française production of Feydeau's *Un fil à la patte*, part of a Peter Daubeny World Theatre Season at the Aldwych. They took one brilliantly contrived farcical situation beyond what one could have believed possible and caused the audience's hysterically mounting laughter to plummet abruptly into distressed silence.

My First Encounter with Theatre-in-the-Round was an early version of Arthur Miller's *Crucible* at Washington Arena Theater, which ever since has messed with my relationship to Proscenium Theatres.

My First Realisation that Theatre could be 'In the Moment', Really and Truly Alive, was Joan Littlewood's *Oh! What a Lovely War* at Stratford East's Theatre Royal. It's the only production – by someone other than myself – I've ever seen more than twice.

The First Play that made me Sweat Profoundly was the original production of *Saved* at the Royal Court. I remember, in the interval, standing on the outside steps, trembling from aftershock and sudden illumination. Sweating was intensified by a production in Tel Aviv of *Execution*, a play by Hanoch Levin, a brilliant, prolific playwright, whose work, sadly, seems to be translator-proof.

My First Experience of the True Meaning of Style and Ensemble was the visit of the Berliner Ensemble to the Old Vic in 1965. I saw five productions on five successive evenings. At long last, I understood! Each production created a Unique World (a word I prefer to style), totally true to itself and totally unlike any of the others. And, what's more – subverting our ideas of how Brecht ought to be done – they were fun, camp even!

The First Productions to Restore My Faith in Theatre after one of my many periods of disillusionment I owe to Robert Lepage: his ninety-minute solo, *Needles and Opium*, and his seven-hour epic, *The Seven Streams of the River Ota*, lifted my theatrical spirits inspiringly skyward.

As a grown-up, I wanted to be a director. My First Production, in Hollywood, was of a one-act play by Tennessee Williams called *Hello from Bertha*, about a whore dying of a broken heart in a New Orleans brothel – a long way from Maida Vale! Nevertheless, it won the Southern California Theatre's Jesse Lasky Award for Best Production. It seemed to confirm me in my third choice of career.

My Last Play…?

Different Every Night (2007), *Then What Happens?* (2013)

Clare Bayley

I was a shy and timid eight-year-old, so although I had the desire, I was overlooked when they were casting the school production of *The Wind in the Willows*. I must have been bold enough to protest, though, because I remember the drama teacher dismissively saying I could audition for the part of Chief Weasel. I think it was intended as a put-down – I was so unlikely to be any good in the role that I would realise my shortcomings and stop bothering her. But in defiance I channelled my drunken inner hellraiser to good effect. I remember the surprise in that drama teacher's eyes. I got the part.

That bit of casting set the pattern for my acting career. At my sixth form, I was Moloch the Magician (in Robert Bolt's best-forgotten *The Thwarting of Baron Bolligrew*), for which my hair had to be plastered down unattractively with baby-oil and the art teacher gave me a zig-zag parting, coloured in with purple eye-liner. I was evil personified and I got to set off coloured flares on stage. My performance was acclaimed.

At university, of course I wanted to play the pretty parts, the heroines, but the competition was too stiff. Eventually I found my way to the inspirational Diane Samuels, who saw something in me and cast me as a Nazi in her play about Hannah Senesh. I also worked with Abigail Morris and the feminist theatre company, Trouble and Strife. We took a devised play about Mary Shelley to Edinburgh. I played Frankenstein's monster.

And through all that of course I learned the lesson that no amount of Juliets or Rosalinds would have taught me – the transgressive fun of stepping into other, bigger, bolder, crueller shoes. That the reason people love theatre, and why it is powerful, is that it allows you to understand someone who you're not.

That, and the companionship of collaborating with a group of other people to pull off a piece of work together – with all the excitement and hilarity and hard work that entails – were the hooks that reeled me in. Then I started going to the theatre. When I was a theatre critic I saw a huge amount of electrifying work. Of all of them the one I can't forget was the Maly Theatre of St Petersburg's *Brothers and Sisters*. It was a long time ago, and what I remember of it may be completely false and distorted. But the memory is so important that even if it is wrong, I still want to hang onto it.

The production was extremely long, and performed in Russian, telling the story of the physical and emotional hardships of life on a collective farm immediately after the Second World War. My overriding memory is of the stoicism and suffering of the women left behind when their men go off to war.

We witness years and years of back-breaking work, sexual frustration and emotional privation, which takes hours and hours for us in the theatre – but it isn't gruelling; it's enthralling, captivating. Eventually, after all those years and all those hours, the news comes that the men are returning. Despite their grief, hunger and exhaustion the women find new energy and put their scant resources into a welcome-home fiesta for the men: bunting, food, drink, music. They gather on stage, waiting for them to arrive. They wait. They hope. From somewhere behind the auditorium, the sound of an approaching marching-band. It grows louder and louder until the jubilant men burst into the auditorium and march triumphantly through the audience, up onto the stage, and are reunited with their womenfolk. There is cheering, hugging, crying, kissing, dancing. The theatre resounds with joy and celebration.

But something isn't quite right. As we watch, the men start to fade away from the stage. The music grinds to a halt, and there are the women again, alone and waiting for their men. And then, again, we hear the marching band, faint at first but getting closer and louder. What's going on? We're confused. We look around the auditorium – has there been some kind of glitch? A catastrophically missed cue?

Then, from the back, a pathetic straggle of wounded men limps and hobbles their way through the audience. There are only a very few of them, and they are old men. They are dirty, ragged and broken, with missing arms and legs, bandages on their heads. Slowly, painfully, they make their way to the women. As they approach, the women realise – as do we in the audience – that this is all that is left to return to them. The first homecoming was their hope, their fantasy. The reality is this: cruel and bitter and full of disappointment.

And that's how the play ended. We stayed in our seats, overwhelmed and crying, until long after the house lights were back on and the cast were off carousing in the bar. The emotion of that *coup de théâtre*, of false hope dramatised, has never left me. We had more than understood something we didn't know before – we had experienced it.

The Enchantment (2007, adapted from Victoria Benedictsson), *The Container* (2007), *Blue Sky* (2012)

Alecky Blythe

The first play I experienced took place in my second-form Speech and Drama class. It was my favourite class, run by the formidable Mrs Blythe. Tall and elegant, and an actress in her youth, she injected into her teaching the same passion and theatricality that I imagine she must have put into every part. She used to ruthlessly critique our poetry recitals, regardless of our delicate age or demeanour. I feared and adored her in equal measure.

One particular week, we were treated to a performance of a Joyce Grenfell monologue from *George, Don't Do That!* by one of the older girls, who was in need of a group of seven-year-olds on whom to rehearse. I sat cross-legged on the floor along with my classmates and listened in wide-eyed wonder. I found myself completely transported to Grenfell's world of naughty children and truly believed I had become one of them. This to me seemed quite different from the poetry recitals I had heard in class before, as this time, even though I was still just listening, I was actively engaged in listening rather than passively, and that was how the spell was cast. When I later discovered that some people made a living out of this magic called 'make-believe', I knew that was what I wanted to do with my life.

Twenty years on, despite not exactly making what anyone could call a living out of it, my childhood dream remained strong. So in the absence of work coming to me, I decided to create my own to appear in. My first play was *Come Out Eli*, inspired by a verbatim workshop run by Mark Wing-Davey at the Actors Centre. I had an idea to make a play about fear, so I ventured out to situations that I hoped would give way to conversations around the subject. As luck would have it, a siege taking hold just round the corner from where I had recently moved to in Hackney provided the perfect setting. Armed with a microphone, a smile and a bucket load of determination, I recorded conversations with curious onlookers, intrigued and perturbed by the police cordon that was infringing on their everyday lives. The police decided not to storm the block of bedsits where Eli Hall, the gunman, was holed up with a hostage, mistakenly thinking he would eventually come out. It was not until fifteen days later that the stand-off ended with a shoot-out between Eli and the police, in which Eli took his own life. During those fifteen days I visited the cordon many times, collecting material that was to document the story of how the immediate community was affected by this extraordinary event.

Once it was over, I visited nearby residents to incorporate their version of events and to fill in some of the gaping holes in my narrative. Most notably, owing to my day job, temping as a receptionist, I had missed its dramatic conclusion, which came to a spectacular climax after Eli's death with the whole block burning down. The final piece of the jigsaw that I needed was an interview with the hostage, who had escaped after eleven days. However, brokering the deal for his payment in return for an interview took the play in a most unexpected direction. Having previously spoken to some of the major papers and channels, which must have rewarded him handsomely financially for his story, the hostage was not willing to talk to me for no fee, as my very limited production budget could not afford one, so he asked me over the phone if I would instead pay by sleeping with him. Not knowing whether I would ever get to meet him for an interview, I recorded my side of the conversations in case these were to be my only contact and insight into this man. Fortunately, we did come to an eventual agreement that involved lunch on me at Wetherspoons, £50 and no sex. The phone encounters provided a most surprising and illuminating opening to the show, allowing the audience a window into the verbatim process and a furtive introduction to the world of the siege.

I don't think Mrs Blythe would have ever imagined where her Speech and Drama classes could lead to, but I hope she would be pleased with the outcome if she had been around to witness it. It strikes me only now that even though on the surface Joyce Grenfell's nursery monologues and a verbatim play about the Hackney siege do not appear to have much in common, they both rely heavily on direct address requiring the very active engagement of the audience, so perhaps verbatim theatre was a natural progression for me. It was only shortly before making *Come Out Eli* that I changed my stage name, adopting my inspirational teacher's, so Mrs Blythe's Speech and Drama classes are never very far from me, and that serves as a great comfort when needed in this precarious business.

Cruising (2006), *The Girlfriend Experience* (2008), *London Road* (2011, with Adam Cork)

Andrew Bovell

My father stood on the station platform waving me goodbye. I was leaving the town I had grown up in and was moving to Melbourne to become a playwright. His eyes misted up as he shook my hand. He was crying. I had never seen him cry before. I didn't quite know what to say, so I lied and said, 'Don't worry. I'll be back soon.'

He took me at my word and waited patiently for my return. He reassured himself that this 'writing caper' would be over soon and that I would come home and get a real job. It wasn't that he disapproved of me wanting to be a writer. It's just that he had never met one and thought it a risky choice for a career. Better not to have such big dreams, he thought. Then you won't be disappointed.

When I had still not returned after four years he thought he should get on a plane and find out what was going on. His visit worried me. I was no longer the boy I was four years ago. Or at least I was trying not to be that boy. There were parts of my life that my father wouldn't approve of. But also, I am ashamed to say, there were parts of my life that wouldn't approve of him.

His visit coincided with the production of my first play. It was a black comedy called *After Dinner* about five lonely and sexually frustrated people looking for a good time on a Friday night out and not succeeding. My father and I had never talked about sex. We had settled into that comfortable position that fathers and their sons often do of avoiding the subject. Unfortunately, my first play talked a great deal about sex and in the most graphic terms.

ANDREW BOVELL

At one point one of the characters described with distaste how her husband woke her in the morning by jabbing his erection into her back. She would lie there with her eyes closed pretending to be asleep until she felt the wet spurt of his ejaculation soak through her nightgown. It was a fairly tragic account of marital intimacy but in the context of the play was also quite funny.

You can't help but reveal yourself when you write a play. Not the biographical detail of your life, but in writing you reveal how you see the world. The young man revealed as the writer of this play was not the son my father knew, and I just wasn't sure how he would respond to this version of me. I was sitting beside him and my eyes slid sideways trying to see the expression on his face. It was contorted. I thought he was in pain, and then I realised he was trying his best not to laugh but in the end couldn't help himself. It's a great joy to cause a theatre full of people to laugh, even more so when one of those people is your father.

I introduced him to the actors and some friends after the show. Being theatre people they all kissed him and hugged him and congratulated him as if he had written the play himself. I even heard him say to someone, 'He must have got his sense of humour from me.' My father was glowing with pride, and I love those friends who made him feel so special that night for being the father of the playwright.

As we walked home from the theatre he told me that he and Mum had sex before they were married. Several times. Perhaps it was the cheap wine after the show or the sexual frankness of the play that had loosened him and prompted this confession, but I felt so gentle toward him, so protective of him at that moment thinking that this was probably the greatest transgression of his life. Perhaps.

I had given him my bed in the house that I shared, and I slept on the floor beside him that night. As we lay there in the dark he said, 'I think you might have something... with this writing caper.' 'Thanks, Dad,' I replied. 'I suppose this means that you won't be coming home.' 'No, I don't think so.' 'Your mother will be disappointed but she'll get used to it.' I knew that my mother had well and truly come to terms with my absence. It was him that was disappointed. That was the way he expressed emotion. Mum was his proxy.

As it turned out, the first play of mine that my father saw was also the last. He did that thing that fathers do to their children. He died before I really got to know him, leaving me with so many unanswered questions. I was too young then and too self-absorbed to know that I even needed to ask them.

Since then I have stood in airport terminals and watched my own children leave for other cities and other lives. And now I know just how my father felt on that day of our first parting, and I'm hoping that I don't die before my children are ready to ask their questions of me.

When the Rain Stops Falling (2009), *Speaking in Tongues* (2009)

Howard Brenton

I wrote my first play when I was eleven.

It was based on a strip character in *The Eagle*, a boy's comic which was launched in 1950. *The Eagle* was a miracle of blazing colour and glorious imagination for kids in the early '50s. On its front and rear covers there was Dan Dare, Pilot of the Future, with his space ship Anastasia and his gang of vivid friends: Digby, the comedian of the crew, Prof. Peabody – a girl! – who was the science officer and Sondar the good Treen, who was the muscle. The Treens were Vesuvian Nazis led by the loathsome genius of The Mekon, a tiny green figure with a very big head who floated around on an anti-gravity boat. Decades later The Mekon morphed into Davos in *Doctor Who*. The Mekon and Dan would have philosophical debates about the meaning of power: 'Death is inevitable, Dare.' I really do think I recall that line! There was a didactic edge to *The Eagle*: it had been founded by a vicar.

But the character I put into a play was not the full-colour Dan Dare but the black and white 'Harris Tweed, Special Agent'. He was a detective on *The Eagle*'s first inside page. A monocled, blazered, pompous buffon, with wonderfully drawn, crinkly Brylcreemed-down hair, Tweed was an hilarious disaster of a detective who got everything wrong. But every week he was rescued from the scrapes he blundered into by the unacknowledged brilliance of his permanent companion, a boy aged… oh yes… about eleven, known only as 'Boy'. Who was he: Harris Tweed's son, his nephew? It was never explained. I suspect this innocent relationship would be impossible to present now.

In 1953 I was living in an Eden called Bognor Regis.

My best friend was called Ralph. His father was a wealthy printer in the town with a fine house; it had leadlight windows, white stuccoed walls and a pond in the front garden that attracted dragonflies. It was to this house my father, mother and sister were invited with other neighbours to watch the Queen's coronation, the first time I ever saw television. I lived in a council house, and my garden was mostly vegetables, but Ralph's garden was a huge hinterland. There were vegetables too – I suspect everyone in the early 1950s grew as much of their own food as they could, still a necessity after the war. But there was also an apple orchard, a big lawn and a wild area at the back overlooking a railway line. It was here Ralph, I and our friends spent many happy hours playing. There was football and cricket of course, but there were also secret projects. We pooled our pocket money and bought an air gun, which we hid in the garden's shed. We shot at green apples on the orchard's trees. We had a grand project: 'the hole'. This we dug at the end of the garden. The idea was to go down far enough to start a tunnel which would go out under Bognor and the sea to France. We covered it up with branches and earth and grass. Our parents were horrified when it was discovered: it was alarmingly deep.

My dad was a keen amateur theatre producer. He used to take the Samuel French editions of the comedies he directed and cover them neatly in brown paper. I was copying him: I wrote my play out in a Woolworth's lined notebook and made a cover. I think the play was probably about three pages long. Then I wrote out parts on separate pages for my friends to act. And it was in Ralph's garden that we performed *Harris Tweed, Special Agent* with our parents as the audience.

I can still see us, at play with my first play, in memory's magic garden.

Diving for Pearls (1989), *H.I.D.* (1989), *Iranian Nights* (1989, with Tariq Ali), *Moscow Gold* (1990, with Tariq Ali), *Berlin Bertie* (1992), *Faust: Parts I & II* (1995, from Goethe), *Hot Irons* (1995), *Ugly Rumours* (1998, with Tariq Ali), *Paul* (2005), *In Extremis* (2006), *Never So Good* (2008), *Anne Boleyn* (2010), *The Ragged Trousered Philanthropists* (2010, adapted from Robert Tressell), *55 Days* (2012), *#aiww: The Arrest of Ai Weiwei* (2013), *Dances of Death* (2013, from Strindberg)

Simon Callow

I was an almost total write-off at drama school in my first year. I scraped through at the end of the year more because of my obvious passion and desperation than because of any evidence of talent or indeed comprehension of the work. Things scarcely improved during my second year, though at least I was less tired thanks to a grant that a kindly ILEA had given me. I was still struggling against a terrible internal block which refused to allow me any sort of free expression: everything I did was controlled to the last degree. I seemed hell-bent on impressing some invisible admirer. I probably seemed very self-satisfied, very confident, but I knew my work was rubbish – knew, not least, because my teachers, with varying degrees of tact, told me so, over and over again. 'Leave yourself alone!' they chanted, almost in unison. It took two liberating experiences to unlock me from the prison in which I had incarcerated myself, to release the emotional life I had so firmly bottled up. The first shock was administered by the great acting teacher, Doreen Cannon, who goaded me – there is no other word – to combustion point during an Extreme Emotion exercise, through which I was sauntering with my customary nonchalance, impersonating, I think, George Sanders or some other unspeakably cool dude. Prodded by Doreen, I finally lost my temper and exploded all over the class. It was profoundly satisfying, the first time, I suspect, ever in my life till that point, that I had dared to give in to an emotion.

Only a few days later, in another class, I was acting in a piece that I had also written and directed, about fourth-century Greece.

Preoccupied with my writerly and directorly responsibilities, I stopped seeing myself from outside, and simply played the character I had given myself, an Ancient Greek Everyman, whom I had roguishly called Testikles. For the first time, the thing I had so strained for over the last eighteen months – to make people laugh – came completely naturally. I was aware of an unaccustomed bodily relaxation, as if an iron cage – a suit of armour, as heavy as it was constricting – had been removed from me. Halfway through the course, I at last felt ready to begin training as an actor.

The first play I did after that was by Feydeau, *Le Dindon*, the play later wittily translated by Peter Hall and Nicki Frei as *An Absolute Turkey*, and I had been given the part of Major Pinchard, who, with his deaf wife, innocently visits the brothel where Act Two is located. It is a secondary part, but the new me fell on it hungrily. No longer out to impress with my control, charm and self-possession, I wanted to give myself over to the character. As always, Feydeau gives you the whole man in a few lines, his passions, his confusions, his contradictions. Pinchard, the military man, when plunged into a scene filled with amorous possibilities, becomes skittish and gallant, but then turns fiercely protective of his unhearing wife. I read everything I could about Feydeau, I studied the cartoons of Sem, the incomparable chronicler of bourgeois life in Belle Epoque Paris, I listened to operettas by Offenbach, Messager, Reynaldo Hahn. I drew on the memories of pre-First World War Paris of my French grandmother and her sister. I found and repaired a uniform for the Major, I purloined my late grandfather's hand stick for him, I made him a kepi from white cardboard and painted it, I grew a moustache and borrowed some moustache wax for it from an old actor friend, for a few shillings I bought a monocle from a bric-a-brac shop in the Vauxhall Bridge Road. I fell in love with Buffy Pinchard, as I called him, and would spend whole days as him, going into the local Chalk Farm shops and placing my order in his impossibly fruity voice.

Rehearsals were, for me, glorious. I felt I had nothing to prove, I simply had to give in to the Pinchard life force. In doing so, I found myself for the first time in my training able to listen to what the other characters were saying, and to be spontaneously astonished or delighted or dismayed by it. The mechanics of the scenes are so meticulously worked out by Feydeau that one simply has to follow his instructions to the letter. If one does, one becomes part of the massive energy he generates; one is swept along by the play's manic imperatives. The laughter that Buffy and his deaf wife, wonderfully impersonated in that production by the statuesque Australian actress Sue Nicholson, was glorious, but it was a bonus. The important thing, the exciting thing, was Being Buffy. I was absolutely at his command.

I'm very much afraid that I've never given a better performance of anything subsequently. The joy of discovery, the freedom, the innocence have all been replaced by something more knowing, more self-conscious, more studiedly skilful. What Dickens called 'the joys of assumption' have never entirely, thank God, deserted me, though that first love affair with Buffy has proved, like all first loves, unreproduceable.

Shooting the Actor (1990), *Love is Where It Falls* (2007), *My Life in Pieces* (2011)

Alexi Kaye Campbell

The first professional job I was offered as an actor was playing a range of characters in an adaptation of Barry Hines' *A Kestrel for a Knave*. It was a production that was to tour schools around France, and, after a year of waiting on tables in London and struggling to get an agent, the prospect of travelling around France and performing a wonderful story excited me hugely. As I packed my bags for Paris I imagined eight months of cafés au lait and croissants, conversations about Racine and Molière with drama students and an endless supply of Gauloises. And, inexplicably, a beige raincoat.

The reality of course was a lot less romantic and a little less clichéd. What I remember from that job was the white van which me and the rest of the company seemed to spend hours and hours loading and unloading or travelling in. There were 5 a.m. starts, screws to be screwed, sound equipment to be packed, costumes to be hung up, motorways to be hurtled along, hordes of loud teenagers to be entertained. Some days we were working for fourteen hours, travelling hundreds of miles and performing three shows before returning to our Parisian base after midnight.

We were an eclectic troupe – British, Greek, Croatian, Norwegian, gay, straight and in-between – and inevitably someone was always playing the guitar. I remember once being pulled over by the police as we hysterically waved our arms around the inside of the van trying to rid it of the aroma of recently smoked marijuana. I also remember a terrible argument somewhere south of Nantes (I think it was about upstaging), and a very sudden peasouper an hour outside Lyon when I thought we would all die in a fireball.

But the thing I remember most was tied up with the very reason I was there – to do what I had always wanted to do with my life, which was to tell stories. And we tried to tell this particular story about hardship, commitment and a big bird with as much passion as we could muster. As we brought our many characters to life – I myself was playing a bullying brother, a delinquent schoolchild, a petty bureaucrat and a sadistic headmaster – we worked hard and wholeheartedly, and it was in that work that I came to learn a lesson about performing stories which would hold me in good stead twenty years later when I turned my hand to playwriting.

And the lesson is this: you cannot fake it. Facing a sea of excitable fifteen-year-olds who were watching a play in a language that wasn't their own, we could not afford to give anything less than everything we had. On the few occasions when for whatever reason we did so – either because of tiredness, bad tempers or laziness – we were quick to know. Suddenly that sea turned against us – it became restless, disrespectful, even mocking – and we were told in no uncertain terms that the failure was ours. Probably the worst thing about those few bad performances was that we had forever planted in certain of those young people's minds the thought that theatre was not essential.

Because on the days when we gave everything that is exactly what theatre felt like – *essential*. A contract between two groups of people – one which was telling a story and the other which was receiving it. That contract demanded an extraordinary generosity on both sides. They were giving us their time, their eyes and their ears, and we were going to give them something which could amuse and intrigue them but also – we hoped – could reflect, elucidate, inspire and move. And when that contract was honoured on both sides and together we walked that knife's edge between this world and another, the result was always magical and always intoxicating.

After those particularly successful performances, the atmosphere in our little white van as we sped back to Paris was always lighter, happier. There was usually some laughter about a prop that had misbehaved or an entrance that was nearly missed, and then the guitar would emerge again and a few strings played. I usually sat in the seat nearest the back with my head against the window pane watching France pass by in the dark. And mostly on those nights I'd be thinking that the choice I had made to follow this path of storytelling was the only one I'd ever want.

The Pride (2008), *Apologia* (2009), *The Faith Machine* (2011), *Bracken Moor* (2013)

Anupama Chandrasekhar

I must have been ten years old when I watched my first play live. It was a Tamil retelling of the ancient Hindu epic, Ramayana – from the point of view of its antagonist, Ravana. It was called *Lankeswaran,* I think. In those days, plays for children were practically unheard of. This one, with its mythological story, its premise of good versus evil and promise of special effects, was deemed suitable for children and hence was an event not to be missed. Also because it was an R.S. Manohar production. Manohar was a thespian Tamil director/actor/producer who staged spectacular mythologicals. I sat in one of the front rows with my grandfather.

Even now I remember my anticipation of the famous scene where the monkey god Hanuman confronts Ravana. Hanuman has been sent by Lord Rama to convey a warning to the King of Lanka. King Ravana, in all his royal arrogance, treats Hanuman as nothing more than an animal and fails to accord him the respect that any royal emissary was entitled to in ancient India. So a miffed Hanuman decides to get even. I knew what came next, and yet I was totally unprepared for it. Hanuman's tail grew and grew and neatly coiled up so he could sit on it at an equal height to Ravana on his throne. I simply couldn't figure out how it was done. The tail seemed like a proper tail and not the coir rope that I'd been expecting, and it seemed to be growing out of Hanuman's butt. I remember standing up on my seat to scan the stage for clues as to how it was done, despite annoyed exclamations from backbenchers. Hanuman, now every inch Ravana's equal, noticed me from his vantage point. He looked at me and grinned for a moment before focusing all attention on the arch villain.

Manohar retired soon after the run. To date, there has been no Tamil director who could match him in those spectacular magic sequences.

Free Outgoing (2007), *Disconnect* (2010)

Caryl Churchill

My first play, the first one I saw, was *Cinderella*. I was three I think. I have a sense of brightness and event, but the only image at all clear is of Buttons in his red clothes. Maybe many people haven't seen a pantomime of Cinderella and don't know how it works. As well as Cinders, Ugly Sisters (men), Fairy Godmother, Prince, there is Dandini, the Prince's friend (I think he rather than the prince is often the Principal Boy, i.e. a girl, or are they traditionally both girls?), and Buttons, a young lad, Cinders' friend, looking like a bellboy, and in love with Cinders though she doesn't know it. I've seen *Cinderella*s since so I don't know what I saw then. But what I did notice was how the panto was put together, scene after exciting scene in different places with characters in different clothes, and Buttons out front entertaining the audience during the scene changes behind the curtain. I can remember doing my own versions with dolls and stuffed animals playing the parts. My parents were the audience, and while I got the dolls into different clothes for the next scene I left a bear alone out front to keep them entertained.

Light Shining in Buckinghamshire (1989), *Traps* (1989), *Cloud Nine* (1989), *Icecream* (1989), *Churchill: Shorts* (1990), *Mad Forest* (1990), *The Skriker* (1994), *Thyestes* (1990, from Seneca), *Hotel* (1997), *This is a Chair* (1997), *Blue Heart* (1997), *Churchill Plays: Three* (1998), *Far Away* (2000), *A Number* (2002), *A Dream Play* (2005, from Strindberg), *Drunk Enough to Say I Love You?* (2006), *Churchill Plays: Four* (2008), *Bliss* (2008, from Olivier Choinière), *Seven Jewish Children* (2009), *Love and Information* (2012), *Ding Dong the Wicked* (2012)

Jo Clifford

My first costume (which I never got) was a set of wings.

I found them in an empty room of the huge rambling old house we lived in when I was a child.

They were so beautiful I didn't dare touch them.

But when a week or so later I desperately wanted to wear them they were gone.

Perhaps I had dreamt them; but I cried and cried because I so wanted them.

I think I wanted to be an angel.

My first part (which I never got) was to be a flower.

It was that or be a gnome.

It was obvious, really. I mean who in their right mind would want to be a gnome?

And I couldn't really understand why, when it came to the flower rehearsals, I was the only boy.

I remember worried grown-up conversations about it all (but why were they so worried?) and somehow the anxiety must have got to me because I came down with mumps.

And never got to be a flower.

My first costume (which I did get) was a very plain yellow dress in a musical whose title I forget in my first boarding school when I was ten.

The dressing room was a dormitory and it smelt of old-fashioned theatre make-up, and I loved that smell, and they played long-playing records of *Gigi* and *High Society* and *My Fair Lady,* and I loved them too.

But I wasn't very good as a musical-comedy actress because my music teacher had managed to convince me I couldn't sing. So I vaguely opened and closed my mouth in time to the music.

I was disappointed in the dress. I wanted something more frilly.

My first proper speaking part was as Sylvia in *One Way Pendulum* in my next boarding school. And the next year I was Lizzie in *Next Time I'll Sing to You.*

I loved rehearsals. I loved working with everyone and I loved the feeling of knowing I belonged.

I loved being Lizzie. I loved the trouser suit I wore and the long blonde wig and the make-up and the feeling of having false eye-lashes.

I felt confident and happy and I wasn't shy any more.

And then my father came to see the second performance and I realised I wanted to be a girl and I felt so frightened and ashamed.

I was terrified that if people got to know who I was they would hate me and make my life a misery and I would die of shame.

I can't really say that was how I discovered I was a transsexual because the word was not then in common use. As far as I could tell, who I was was something unspeakable.

And I can't really say that was when I discovered theatre was my artistic and spiritual home, although looking back on it it's very clear I did, because at the time theatre became a place of fear and terror and the deepest shame.

And that was why finding my voice in the theatre took me twenty years.

My first original theatre play was *Losing Venice* in 1985.

My first publisher was dear lovely Nick Hern, who published it.

The first time I read a Calderón was *La vida es sueño* in 1965. And the first time I translated it was for Calixto Bieito and the Edinburgh International Festival in 1998.

(And that was a dream come true.)

The first time I was in a film was in Gateway Films' *God's New Frock* in 2003.

(And now I so love being in films.)

The first time I understood how much it mattered that I'm a transsexual playwright was in a conference in 2004. I'd always thought that what makes my work so distinctive was the fact that I had steeped myself in Golden Age Spanish plays when I was young. But at that conference, and my dearly beloved partner Susie slowly dying of a brain tumour, and me half out of my mind with pain and strain and grief, I found myself unexpectedly saying 'I'm not a male playwright, and I'm not a female playwright. I'm a transgendered playwright', and I suddenly realised what an amazing gift and privilege that is.

The first time I had three hundred people picketing one of my plays was when fundamentalist Christians demonstrated outside my *Gospel According to Jesus Queen of Heaven* in the Tron Theatre in Glasgay in 2009.

My adolescent fears had come true. They did know who I was and they did hate me for it.

But I survived.

The first play I had published under my woman's name was, I think, *Every One* at the Edinburgh Lyceum in 2010.

I know that was the first time I sat and listened to the audience's intent deep silence and realised that the funny sniffling noise was people crying.

The first time I acted in a play with another actor, and got paid for it, was *Sex Chips and the Holy Ghost* in Òran Mór with David Walshe in 2012.

(Forty-seven years after *Next Time I'll Sing to You*.)

The first time I had a play on in the West End was *Great Expectations* in 2013 at the Vaudeville Theatre. I am the first openly transsexual woman playwright to have a play on in the West End, and proud of that.

(And proud to have said so in the film of the production, and to have pointed out that when I first wrote that play in 1988 I was a shy youngish man. And that now I'm a grandma.)

The first time I acted in an outdoor production was yesterday. On Easter Sunday. In Theatre Alba's passion play.

I tried to stop my teeth chattering in the bitter Edinburgh wind and told Mary Magdalene there is no need to weep.

And there isn't any, it's true, and no need to mourn either: because at last I was playing an angel.

It's true I still didn't have any wings. And that it's taken almost sixty years.

But you can't have everything.

And next time I will have wings.

Losing Venice (1990), *Ines de Castro* (1990), *Light in the Village* (1991), *Bazaar* (1997, from David Planell), *Life is a Dream* (1998, from Calderón), *Celestina* (2004, from de Rojas), *Faust: Parts I & II* (2006, from Goethe), *Blood Wedding* (2008, from Lorca), *Every One* (2010), *Yerma* (2010, from Lorca), *The Tree of Knowledge* (2011), *The House of Bernarda Alba* (2012, from Lorca), *Great Expectations* (2012, adapted from Dickens)

Dominic Cooke

The first play I directed was *Tissue* by Louise Page. It's a com-
pressed, impressionistic play about a young woman's experience
of breast cancer. It's written in multiple scenes, with numerous
characters played by three actors.

I did the play in my second year at Warwick University with a
group I'd formed with some friends the previous summer called
Glamorous Grannies Ents Co-op. Our first production had been
Joe Orton's *The Erpingham Camp*, in which I'd played Chief
Redcoat Reilly. To pay for the Orton we'd each put in a fiver, and
the show made some money, allowing us to produce
Tissue out of the profits. After *Tissue*, we blew all the money on a
production of Edward Bond's *The Sea*, in which I played the
draper, Hatch, and had to be taken to casualty in the tech, having
cut my finger open. When Hatch goes mad he stabs a dead body
on the beach, and I'd had the ingenious idea of using a real knife.
So much for verisimilitude in the theatre.

We performed *Tissue* in the university chaplaincy. The cast
included Ruth Jones, who remains one of the most exceptional
actors I've worked with and who I formed a theatre company with
when we left university. Alongside Ruth was my best mate Dave
and, in the main part of Sally, another fantastic actress called
Clare, who now works as a clown. It was a very spare production.
We had no props, no costume changes and the set was three polystyrene blocks which we moved to create the environment for
each scene. I had no idea what I was doing, but my actors were

inventive and the simplicity of the production suited the play. After the first performance I hid, so as to avoid the audience's inevitable scorn, but a fellow student called Aileen, who I didn't know that well, found me and told me that she'd liked it. I was over the moon.

If I hadn't have done this production, I don't think I'd be a director now. The space given to young people at university to follow their passions is so important, and I was privileged to be in a generation where we were given full grants and had our fees paid. I feel lucky to have had the freedom of my student years.

Arabian Nights (1998, 2009), *Noughts & Crosses* (2007, adapted from Malorie Blackman)

Oliver Ford Davies

Richard II seems to have haunted me most of my life. In 1948 my father took me to see Shakespeare's play at His Majesty's Theatre in the Haymarket: it was a Stratford transfer starring Robert Harris. I was eight, a curious parental choice for my first Shakespeare. I was entranced by two things, the armour and the Groom. I imagined clanking about in full armour would be the acme of delight, and visiting a desolate king in prison would be the most romantic thing imaginable, and if the Groom did put his foot in it by saying how proudly roan Barbary had carried Bolingbroke at his coronation that made him all the more human – certainly something an eight-year-old could relate to.

Perhaps therefore it was no coincidence that reading history at Oxford I chose Richard II as my special subject. Basically if you can wade through a thousand pages of medieval Latin you know more or less everything there is to know about the king, and you discover, inevitably, how slanted Shakespeare's play is. I have wanted to rewrite the first act ever since, to explain why he exiles Mowbray and Bolingbroke – Shakespeare just doesn't care about backstories. When I left academic teaching, my first professional job at the old Birmingham Rep, aged twenty-seven, was to understudy the director Peter Dews as John of Gaunt, and to play Salisbury and… the Groom. After ten days we had a run-through of the first half, with Peter out front and me deputising as Gaunt. At notes, Peter announced: 'Oliver is a total bastard and he's playing Gaunt – I'm not competing with that – but he's still got to play Salisbury and the Groom.' It remains, I imagine, a unique treble, since the chief attraction of Gaunt, apart from *the* speech, is that you can go home after forty-five minutes. In an effort to differentiate the three parts, I ended up playing the Groom in a high-pitched cockney, a performance I look back on with total embarrassment. The Groom had lost its allure.

In 1975 I joined the RSC, and in *Henry IV, Part 1* I played an assortment of small parts and understudied Emrys James as Henry IV. My sixth, or possibly seventh, appearance was as a decoy king at the Battle of Shrewsbury. I had just played Sir Michael, so it involved getting into full armour in ninety seconds and clanking about the field unconvincingly brandishing my sword, while Alan Howard and Brewster Mason enjoyed themselves. How I hated the whole thing but... I was at last cured of both the Groom and full armour. In autumn 2013 I am going back to the RSC to play the Duke of York in Greg Doran's production of *Richard II*, sixty-five years after my first encounter with the play. But I've checked: the Duke can't double with the Groom, and since he 'remains as neuter' in the conflict he can't be wearing armour.

Playing Lear (2003), *Performing Shakespeare* (2007)

Gregory Doran

A Midsummer Night's Dream was the first play I ever directed professionally, but it was also the first play I ever heard.

My dad was part of a record club. In the post one day, at our home just outside Preston, a box of Beethoven symphonies arrived. Along with it came a 45rpm record of Mendelssohn's miraculous incidental music to *A Midsummer Night's Dream*. From the moment those first four evocative chords sounded, I was hooked. I could see the fairies rushing in on a breeze, like leaves being scurried across a lawn. I could picture Bottom hee-hawing, and the rude mechanicals thumping about in the earthy brass fortissimo.

But in between the musical sections, my record had extracts from the actual play itself. And as Shakespeare instructs, I attended 'with patient ears', as this magical story unfolded. It was an American production, and the actress playing Puck sounded to my young ears just like Mickey Mouse. But when she squeaked 'I'll put a girdle round about the Earth in forty minutes' I caught my breath.

Just before I was born, the Russians had launched the first satellite, triggering the Space Age which obsessed my childhood. Sputnik, as this satellite was called, could orbit the Globe in just over an hour and a half. So Puck was twice as fast as Sputnik!

A Midsummer Night's Dream has always had the ability to capture and tangle the imagination, like any good dream. It contains some of the most beautiful poetry in the English language, or I would vouch, in any language on earth. And it must be the most deliriously funny play ever written, yet so much of the story seems deadly serious, and at times hardly the most fitting introduction to Shakespeare for young people.

When I was still a student at Bristol, in 1982, I got the opportunity to direct the play at a community college in Jamestown, in upstate New York. And as I was paid for the job, I regard it as my first play as a professional director.

There was a daunting moment on the first day of rehearsals when a student approached me tapping his copy of the text:

– 'This play, he enquired, *A Midsummer Night's Dream*? It's by William Shakespeare?'

– 'Yes,' I replied a little warily, 'Why?'

– 'See, it says on the cover it's by Pelican Shakespeare.'

But the students' unfamiliarity with the play allowed them to approach it without preconceptions, and indeed to take it very seriously indeed. Only when they got it in front of an audience did they realise just how funny it was.

At a seminar on the play, during rehearsals, one of the tutors (in what I think was called the Human Potential Center) objected that the choice of play was surely inappropriate for the students, as the plot revolved around a jealous husband who drugged his wife and subjected her to sexual congress with a donkey.

Hermia is condemned either to death, or to incarceration in a convent if she disobeys her father. Quince and his little acting troop are terrified that they will be hanged if their play frightens the ladies at court, and, later, they see their friend Bottom horribly transformed into an ass. The lovers, lost in the dark wood, lose any sense of civil behaviour and debase themselves in bouts of furious brawling. This is surely the stuff of nightmares not dreams.

But then the title of the play itself may have misled us.

Before I directed the play at Stratford for the Royal Shakespeare Company, in 2005, I decided to research that title a little more deeply. Apparently, for the Elizabethans, the period known as midsummer was not the idyllic time of year that we now associate with late June, with evenings stretching ever longer, a time of ease, of strawberries, Pimm's and Wimbledon. For them, it was a dangerous time. The crops were in the field, but had not yet ripened, and if bad weather followed, the harvest would be threatened, which in turn might lead to rising prices, rural discontent and corn riots.

So every precaution had to be taken to propitiate the old Gods. If poppies appeared in the fields, they were regarded as an excellent sign, like blood spattered in sacrifice to protect the harvest.

On the eve of St John's Day, it was thought, a portal opened up between the mortal and the fairy world, and for the next few days, until St Peter's Day, fairies would flood the land creating havoc. Folk would hang garlands of midsummer flowers: vervain, corn marigolds and St John's wort, around the byres of their cattle, or the cradles of their children so the fairies would not swap them for changelings.

And yet, for all this, *A Midsummer Night's Dream* resolves in a benediction of pure joy. Perhaps, as John Mortimer once said, 'Comedy is just Tragedy speeded up.'

I made a final discovery about the play's title when I was on tour with the RSC in Washington and visited the Folger Library. They have in their possession Trevelyon's Miscellany of 1608. In this hand-drawn book of marvels, the author marks the times the sun rises and sets each day. But he also makes careful note about how long the twilight lasts, and what time it gets light in the morning, or day breaks, before the sun actually appears.

On Midsummer's Eve he writes, 'The sun setteth at twelve minutes past eight, but twilight may last until twenty-four minutes past ten. The day breaketh at thirty-six minutes past one, with the sun rising at forty-seven minutes past three.' So, the actual darkness on Midsummer night lasts a mere three hours and twelve minutes, or roughly the stage running time of *A Midsummer Night's Dream*.

The play continues to enchant my imagination since that first magical encounter, several decades ago.

Cardenio (2011, after Lewis Theobald, after Shakespeare?), *Shakespeare's Lost Play: In Search of Cardenio* (2012)

Ariel Dorfman

It is so far back that I can barely remember the circumstances and certainly not its name, but yes, thinking gently, thinking furiously, I do, I do remember my first play. It had its world premiere in front of an international audience, young and old, in the late spring of 1948, or perhaps it was summer by then. Though the city was New York, this work of my febrile imagination did not have its one and only performance on Broadway, but rather in a modest neighbourhood in Queens.

I was five years old, perhaps just six, and did not yet know how to read or write or even spell my name, but I did have an overflowing need to communicate and tell stories. And because I was an Attention Deficit Disorder child, with much more energy than could fit in one small body, my parents had discovered that the only way to keep me fixed to one spot was to put a sheet of paper on the floor and crayons in my hand and, miracle of miracles, the wild boy would spend several quiet hours drawing pictures.

It's not clear when I decided to draw a series of consecutive scenes and turn them into an overarching sequence. I can't even recall the protagonists of the drama that was spilling out of me like a torrent. I had never seen a play as such before, had not gone to the cinema, nor seen even one television show. I was spurred by the story-books read to me and also by the funnies in the *New York Herald Tribune*. Every Sunday, I would curl up on the rug of our living-dining room with the comics spread out and watch them come alive, animated through actors on the radio impersonating the characters. If I can't evoke the precise heroes of my own first play, I don't doubt that there were cavalcades of them, a gigantic mishmash deriving from variegated fictional universes; so I wouldn't be surprised if that epic I staged was peopled by pirates and knights errant (oh, Prince Valiant) and definitely cowboys and Indians. And there must have been some quest, some struggle for justice, because from an early age that was one of my major obsessions, the sense that something was wrong and unfair in the world, that something had to be done to make things right.

At any rate, at some point, when the drawings had spooled out into ten or fifteen different scenes, and come, I suppose, to a conclusion of sorts, I asked my mother for a large cardboard box. She helped me to cut out a hole in one of the walls of the container, large enough so that the drawings could be seen by an audience and small enough so that they would not realise that it was my hand slipping those pictures in and out of the opening. Nor, I hoped, would they understand that all those voices were my voice, fraudulently deep or falsetto high, playing all the roles and also humming the music, though I had contemplated putting on some records on a little blue record player that was my pride and joy. But I decided against that sort of musical accompaniment. I had enough multi-tasks to juggle, what with the drawings and the voices and, of course, the marketing. Ever the little exhibitionist, I wanted to make sure, after all, that not only my sister and parents would attend the enactment.

I drew dozens of invitations on cards and had my father scribble out time and address as well as the name of the play (how I wish I could remember what it was called!); after which several buddies helped me to deliver news of the performance to an array of residences in our vicinity.

Bizarrely enough, many adults showed up, either because they were towed there by their kids or out of devotion to my father, who was their work colleague at the recently formed United Nations. That's why their families and mine lived in Queens, at Parkway Village, which had been built in order to house the first functionaries of the UN, whose temporary headquarters were in nearby Lake Success. That's why the first audience of my life was so international, perhaps creating inside me the assumption that it was natural that my words should reach across boundaries and countries and creeds. Just as my first playmates were from all the continents and spoke with every conceivable accent at home. The architecture of Parkway Village facilitated this interaction, by creating vast, grass-covered backyards separating the buildings, a space where different people could meet and cohabitate and weave a community, like a Mini-United Nations for everyday existence. And an ideal setting for an open-air spectacle.

So I peered out onto that backyard where every chair and stool in our house and several other houses had been settled on the lawn and saw many colours of skin and heard many tongues chattering to each other in who knows what languages, though I knew that they all shared English as a lingua franca and thus would appreciate my story. They also shared the near universal belief, as I did, that if you liked something you were supposed to applaud.

I wish I could report that my *opera prima* got a standing ovation, but my memory simply refuses to cooperate. I do remember that many of the spectators came up after the show to tell me how much they had enjoyed it, and that I should persevere.

Did that resolutely set me on the path to *Death and the Maiden* and *Widows* and *Purgatorio*?

Probably not. The theatrical impulse discovered in a backyard at Parkway Village needed to be stimulated and completed by Shakespeare and Molière, Pinter and Miller, Antigone and Medea and a family looking out onto a Cherry Orchard as it is felled; there were many mentors and models and other plays waiting on the horizon. And waiting in the wings as well, of course, was life, waiting to teach me some lessons about exile and creativity, repression and resistance and hope. I still had to understand fully that art could be, at the very least, a consolation for the grief and a road to resurrection in the eyes and ears of others. And waiting was the love of my life, Angélica, who was to inspire and encourage all the plays I would write in the future, and may have at that very childish moment been smiling from afar in Chile, because she somehow knew that the Ariel she had yet to meet thirteen years later would nevertheless have wanted her to be there next to him during his first public presentation.

What remains, then, of that nameless play, the one composed only of drawings and performed without a live actor for an audience that has long since disappeared?

The drawings themselves have disappeared as well. They were preserved by my parents for decades only to ultimately be swallowed up by the 1973 coup in Chile.

But this much is true today: I still carry the enthusiasm, if not the energy, of that little boy.

And I still believe, oh yes, that it matters to tell stories, that we cannot survive without the blessings of our compassionate imagination.

Death and the Maiden (1991), *Reader* (1995), *Widows* (1997), *The Resistance Trilogy* (1998), *Purgatorio* (2006)

David Edgar

I became a playwright by a process of elimination which became the stuff of family legend. My parents first met, as young actor stage managers, on the stage-door steps of the Birmingham Repertory Theatre. They took me to my first theatre play, *Beauty and the Beast*, at the age of nearly four, and, at the first entrance of the masked and fearsome creature, I screamed the place down. Eventually, my behaviour became so disruptive that I had to be removed from the auditorium, and as, conveniently, my aunt was administrator of the theatre, I was escorted backstage to meet the now maskless beast in his dressing room, to shake his hand, to watch him put his mask on again, to shake his hand a second time, and to be taken back into the auditorium. Thus reassured, on his next entrance I screamed the place down.

I have had good experiences in the theatre since, but none quite like that. A year later I went to the same playhouse to see the same author's *Tinder Box* – a play full of sinister witches and huge dogs. But this time I was wise. I'd realised it was illusion. And I'd realised also that there was nothing in the world I wanted to do more than help to make those illusions. From the day the magic died – or more accurately, the day I realised that it *was* magic – I wanted to be up there with the magicians.

Between the ages of thirteen and nineteen, however, I found my ambitions somewhat narrowed. Following a disastrous school performance as Miss Prism in *The Importance of Being Earnest* – personally I've always blamed the shoes – my mother concluded,

'Well, it's not going to be acting, is it, dear.' In subsequent years I realised – or was informed – that despite a fine, brown set for *Henry IV, Part 1* it was unlikely to be designing either. My equally brown set for my own school production of *Mother Courage* (precocious, moi?) persuaded me my future was as a director, an illusion which was shattered too by a disastrous student production of *Salome*. I love Wilde, but he put paid to both my acting and my directing ambitions. As editor of the student newspaper – at the height of the 1968 student revolt – I decided I wanted to be writer. And when I left university, even more when I left a short career in journalism three years later, I decided that that mission was best pursued not just by writing, but by writing in the theatre.

Commissioned and first presented by Chris Parr at Bradford University, my first non-student play was professionally premiered in a basement lunchtime theatre in Soho on decimalisation day, 15 February 1971. That my first play was written for two women was a deliberate decision, to avoid what then seemed (and still seems) the danger of autobiographical writing. Nonetheless, *Two Kinds of Angel* remains an indelible part of my autobiography.

Edgar: Shorts (1989), *The Shape of the Table* (1990), *Pentecost* (1995), *Dr Jekyll and Mr Hyde* (1996, adapted from Robert Louis Stevenson), *Albert Speer* (2000), *The Prisoner's Dilemma* (2001), *Continental Divide* (2004), *Playing with Fire* (2005), *A Time to Keep* (2007, with Stephanie Dale), *Testing the Echo* (2008), *How Plays Work* (2009), *Arthur & George* (2010, adapted from Julian Barnes), *The Master Builder* (2010, from Ibsen), *Written on the Heart* (2011), *If Only* (2013)

Helen Edmundson

I wrote my first play at primary school and coerced some friends into performing it with me for the infants. The script hasn't survived. (Sorry, Nick.) Once we got to the end of the text as written, I decided it was going so well that we shouldn't stop, and insisted we all improvise on through more extraordinary twists and turns of plot. My main memory is of a crowd of anxious mothers, their faces pressed up against the windows of the school hall, wondering when they might be able to take their children home, and the amused but besieged teachers desperately signalling to me to make it stop. In the end, they had to intervene.

When I was growing up, my family didn't go to the theatre – unless Danny La Rue was in pantomime. So the first time I saw a proper play was on a sixth-form trip to the RSC in Stratford. It was Michael Pennington in *Hamlet*. I was completely overwhelmed and transformed. After that, I spent most lunchtimes in the dusty wilderness that was the 'School Library', reading my way through the small section of plays. I began with T.S. Eliot and then moved on to George Bernard Shaw. And on my eighteenth birthday, a lady who lived across the road gave me a Complete Works of Shakespeare which kept me going for several months. I was nothing if not thorough.

The first play I acted in at university was my fellow-student Polly Teale's first play, *Jasmine and Violet*, a precociously well-structured exploration of sibling relationships and alter egos. For the performance, she transformed a small grassy area outside the Drama

Department into a perfect amphitheatre and strung fairy lights in the trees. I played Violet's spirit. There was a great deal of mirroring and expressing the underneath involved. 'Violet' and I remain close friends – we bonded over a shared susceptibility to corpsing. After that, I wanted to act in anything and everything, and Polly's exemplary drive inspired me to get on with writing my own material.

The first play I had published was *The Clearing*. The Bush Theatre, under Dominic Dromgoole, had taken the initiative and started selling photocopied, pamphlet-style copies of the plays they were producing. They were flimsy, but they had their own ISBNs. I loved the idea that people might want to own and read some of my words. Not long after that, NHB started to publish my work. I still look forward to the parcel of texts, and Nick's scrawled, handwritten notes. The productions end, but the playtexts are still there. I'm grateful for that.

The Clearing (1994), *The Mill on the Floss* (1994, adapted from George Eliot), *Anna Karenina* (1994, 2011, adapted from Tolstoy), *War and Peace* (1996, 2008, adapted from Tolstoy), *Mother Teresa is Dead* (2002), *Gone to Earth* (2004, adapted from Mary Webb), *Coram Boy* (2005, adapted from Jamila Gavin), *Orestes* (2006), *Life is a Dream* (2009, adapted from Calderón), *Swallows and Amazons* (2011, with Neil Hannon, adapted from Arthur Ransome), *The Heresy of Love* (2012), *Mary Shelley* (2012)

Kevin Elyot

In August 1965, David Warner, long-haired and lanky, slouched onto the stage of the Royal Shakespeare Theatre as Hamlet, swathed in a long woollen scarf, and established yet another high point of arguably one of the finest decades in the company's history.

Set in period, Peter Hall's casting of Warner made it absolutely of its time, and although his look, demeanour and delivery were utterly distinctive, the performance was essentially of the world Hall had created; the play was indeed the thing. For a stage-struck teenager, it was pretty electrifying.

My Night with Reg (1994), *The Day I Stood Still* (1998), *Mouth to Mouth* (2001), *Elyot: Four Plays* (2004), *Forty Winks* (2004)

Richard Eyre

The first play I performed in was *A Midsummer Night's Dream*. I was Peaseblossom in an open-air performance at my primary school and I was six. I remember it only for Puck's habit of bursting into tears whenever she forgot her lines and for making me aware how difficult it is to sustain dramatic illusion against the intrusion of real life. During our scene with Bottom, who wore a rather notional ass's head, a horse that had up till now been quietly and disinterestedly grazing in a field beyond our stage opened a gate and strolled towards Bottom with a speculatively seductive air. There was a great deal of screaming from the cast and the audience and a satisfying descent into chaos.

The first play I saw was at the age of sixteen. It was *Hamlet*. I'd grown up in Dorset, where there were no theatres, and at school I was more interested in maths and physics. But I went to stay with a friend in Bristol, went to the Bristol Old Vic and saw *Hamlet*, which was played by Peter O'Toole in his unreconstructed state – dark-haired, wild, violent, mercurial and thrilling – before stardom and Lawrence of Arabia turned him blond and small-nosed. I had never read the play, barely knew of its existence, and it capsized me. I was like Berlioz, who said, after seeing a performance of the same play in Paris: 'Shakespeare, coming on me unawares, struck me like a thunderbolt. The lightning flash of that discovery revealed to me at a stroke the whole heaven of art, illuminating it to its remotest corners. I recognised the meaning of grandeur, beauty, dramatic truth… I saw, I understood, I felt… that I was alive and that I must arise and walk.' And he added: '…at this time of my life I neither spoke nor understood a word of English.'

The first play I wrote was an adaptation of a novel called *The Ha-Ha* by Jennifer Dawson. It played at the Lyceum Theatre, Edinburgh, and the Hampstead Theatre Club. It was produced by Michael Codron, who, with perfect symmetry, produced the play I've just directed: *Quartermaine's Terms*. Later I wrote an original play, which I withdrew from production after a loss of nerve. Since then, in spite of trying, I've only written adaptations, the last two – *Hedda Gabler* and *Ghosts* – published by Nick Hern.

The first play I directed was Ann Jellicoe's *The Knack*, for one Sunday night during the run of *The Boy Friend*, in which I was appearing at the Phoenix Theatre, Leicester. The ensemble – or at least the male half – used to sit motionless in our dressing room before the show, our feet on the table, staring inscrutably at ourselves and our colleagues out of the corners of our eyes. The challenge was to see who could be the last to get changed, made-up and get on stage for the first bar of the opening number. It was often the first note of the shortish overture that signalled an explosion of activity, with a degree of manic energy and commitment that disappeared as soon as we arrived on stage in our white shirts, trousers and deck shoes and told the audience that it was 'Nicer, much nicer in Nice'. Given our views on Leicester, we could have sung that it was nicer in Anchorage, Alaska, with as much conviction. The play I directed was cast from my fellow actors. After the performance, Clive Perry, the director of the theatre, said this to me: 'If you want to be a director, you can become one. I'm not sure you'll ever be an actor. But you must choose.' And I did.

Hedda Gabler (2005, from Ibsen), *Talking Theatre* (2009), *Ghosts* (2013, from Ibsen)

Stella Feehily

The first play that ever I saw was on the day of my Confirmation. The act of Confirmation means that the Holy Spirit has entered your life – so, to a child with an overactive imagination, it felt like rather a responsibility. My mother sought to alleviate this burden by taking my brother and me to *Mungo's Mansion* by Walter Macken. It premiered at the Abbey Theatre in 1946, and we saw it performed by Bundoran Amateur Players in 1981 at St Patrick Hall, some thirty-five years after its first performance.

The play is set in Galway and concerns the residents of a tenement hoping to move out to the fresh air of a new estate. The characters are spectacularly named: Mungo King, Mowleogs and Winnie the Wild Duck. I only remember that I laughed, and loved it, and marvelled at Tom Walsh, a sober schoolmaster at St Macartan's National School, playing the most extraordinary, thick-accented Galway fellow. It was my first lesson in theatre:

On the stage you can be someone else.

The first play I ever performed in was, of course, a nativity play. I was six and cast as an angel. I was completely fucked off because I was desperate to play Mary, who was by far the best part. When it came to my big moment to say, 'Behold the baby Jesus', I opened my mouth and simply burped. The audience laughed. I was mortified. However, I got a round of applause when I got the line out. The lesson in theatre:

Audiences like it when something goes wrong.

The first play that absolutely blew me away was Wilson Milam's 2002 production of A *Lie of the Mind* – Sam Shepard's violent, sprawling, family drama set in the American West. Catherine McCormack's battered, brain-damaged Beth is still one of the finest performances I have ever seen. The lesson?

A good play can be transformed into a great play with the right actors.

There are certain things in the theatre that are completely real and powerful in themselves. A cascade of water, kissing and, of course, nudity.

I should have remembered this after seeing Joe Dowling's production of *Borstal Boy* by Brendan Behan, which contains a scene of naked young men in a line. On these occasions, you do try to listen to the dialogue and look determinedly at the actors' faces, but after the initial shock, invariably the eye is drawn to the various size and shape of privates on display…

But I wasn't prepared for the nightly gasp from the audience watching *Duck,* my first play, beautifully directed by Max Stafford-Clark. Cat (Duck) is seen at the top of the second act naked in a bath with her older lover. This is followed by a scene where she is nearly drowned by her boyfriend Mark, and then, in a third consecutive scene, Cat emerges like Venus from a council-estate bathtub. During the ducking, the water splashed high across the back stage wall of the Royal Court catching the light iridescently. The utterly gorgeous and talented Ruth Negga suffered a couple of ear infections from this ducking she endured every night. Her doctor inquired if she was a swimming champion. Also, sometimes the water was too hot, which I noted by her scalded-looking legs and sometimes it was too cold: she was shaking. The lesson is:

Leave the torture of actors to Beckett.

The first play that I wish I'd written is *Conversations on a Homecoming* by the great Irish playwright Tom Murphy. I saw it at the Abbey Theatre in 1993 and again at Hampstead Theatre in 2012, both times sublimely directed by Garry Hynes.

The play conjures up a world of loss, longing, failure and myth. It is set in a country bar, where the locals meet, josh and seethe into their pints of plain and whiskey chasers, and the returning emigrant is greeted with thinly disguised resentment.

It made me think of my father and all the Irish who emigrated to England in the 1950s. My father left school in 1948 at the age of nine because of the battering he received at the hands of the Christian Brothers. He went to London at fifteen and returned to Ireland in the late '70s, with money in his pocket, a pretty wife and two kids in tow – having, to all intents and purposes, 'made it'. Considering the poverty he had come from, he had certainly done well enough.

Murphy's play was written in 1985 and is set in the '70s. I recognised his characters, from the country pubs my father took me to. I knew these hard drinkers, the pub wit, the beady whiskey philosophers.

Murphy skewers the pride and shame of small-town life. He writes of an Irish loathing and an Irish self-loathing. I know it: I've felt it, I've seen it.

The final lesson is that great plays teach us things about ourselves we half know but don't dare to articulate, and, importantly, they can also reveal to us our own humanity.

Duck (2003), *O Go My Man* (2006), *Dreams of Violence* (2009), *Bang Bang Bang* (2011)

Vivienne Franzmann

I was watching a pantomime of *Mother Goose* at our local am-dram group when they called for volunteers in the audience to go on stage to sing a song or do a dance. I was four, and I was sitting on my dad's lap when the call came. He says he looked down and I was gone, and the next thing he knew, he saw me charging my way on to the stage ready for my theatrical debut.

When I was about thirteen, my mum took me to see a production of *Waiting for Godot*. I'd never heard of it. I was completely out of my depth. I thought my mum was completely mental and was peeved that she'd dragged me away from *Brookside* to watch a play where nothing happened.

I was floored by a production of *Bent* at the National in my late teens. I found it unbearably moving and I felt the power of theatre for the first time.

When I was at university, I saw Jim Cartwright's *Two*, which I remember the audience loving. What really struck me was the simplicity of the storytelling; how the play respected the audience yet was accessible. I loved its earthiness and how it was hilarious and so sad. It all added up to a very satisfying theatrical experience.

The play that stopped any ambitions I had to be an actor was *Marat/Sade*. I played the part of Marat. I had to paint my face with Copydex glue every night to look like a skin disease. I remember feeling sick with nerves, worried about my pyjamas falling down with rubbery glue hanging off my face thinking, 'Why am I putting myself through this?'

Out of Joint's *Macbeth* was the first time I found a Shakespeare play thrilling. I took a group of sixth-formers to see it, and if you've ever taken a group of teenagers to the theatre, you'll know how hard it is to impress/excite (never mind thrill) them. Set in a war-torn, unspecified African state, it took you right to the heart of the play, slapped you about a bit and spat you out the other end.

When I read Sarah Kane's *4.48 Psychosis*, I thought my heart was going to stop. I've never read a play before or since that left me gasping for air like this did.

I knew I had a play in me and that play turned out to be *Mogadishu*. In 2008, I was heaving my way through my twelfth year of drama teaching when I found out I was one of the Bruntwood prizewinners. And that was when I became a writer.

Mogadishu (2011), *The Witness* (2012)

Stacey Gregg

I'm wearing a wine leather jacket from the market and I fancy a boy wearing a hoody emblazoned with the capitalised word 'FUCK'. I'm at the Lyric Theatre in Belfast, and this is the first and one of scant few times I'll see theatre before I'm twenty, despite being certain since the age of ten that I will be a child star and they will cast me opposite Macaulay Culkin in the next *My Girl* movie. I sent a letter to *Going Live!* explaining this to them. They did not reply.

I'm here to see *Macbeth* and trying to be sophisticated, because these kids go to the swishy school where they go to theatre, and I'm styling it out by acting the eejit to anyone in authority. *Macbeth* is riddled with Norn Irish accents and I hate it. Pah. They don't sound like Shakespeare. It'll take me many more years to understand the complex associations we have with received pronunciation equating to power and accomplishment, whilst skivvies and fools have regional accents.

I'm at university and I don't get the Greek Tragedy paper. I find copies of *Oedipus the King* and *Oedipus Tyrannus*, but I can't find *Oedipus Rex*. Why do people think that's funny? (Answer: they're all the same play. That is quite funny.) I read Steven Berkoff's *Greek* and Sarah Kane's *Phaedra's Love* back to back as a way in to the Greeks, and I still remember slamming them down dramatically next to my pride-of-place green cafetière in my student room. WHY had no one told me of these plays before? These are the first plays that set me buzzing on a new course, and I share

58

them at every opportunity. Within a few months I direct my first play, *Marat/Sade*, in a twelfth-century building. Our over-enthusiastic stage manager puts raw sausages in a scene where we inmates decimate a beheaded corpse: the realisation mid-show that there is lots of dead pig in my hair and I am wearing a strait-jacket and so can do nothing about it is one of my most treasured memories.

I'm doing my finals and my granny passes away. I go home for the wake. I can't put together the loss of a matriarch known in her time as Hatchet Jinny (a clue as to how she would solve problems) with the knowledge that my mates are currently sipping wine by the river in the sun, dreaming of careers. During that summer, while working as security (haha) and before getting fired, I write my first play: it's a version of the Greek Antigone myth, set in my Belfast. It's messy and grieving and angry and one of the most honest things I've ever created. I worry it's a bit nuts, but in Berlin the following year I see a production where a man wriggles on his face, naked, bare bum o'clock, doused in blood, from one end of the stage to another over the duration of about an hour. I'm in love. I'm starry-eyed. I'm somewhere else. And I'll spend a lot of time chasing that buzz, that odd occasion when the clouds part, and a slice of awesomeness beams into your brain and burns a whole new world of possibility.

Perve (2011), *Lagan* (2011), *When Cows Go Boom* (2013)

Catherine Grosvenor

I came to the theatre gradually. I wrote short stories as a child, and I acted in a variety of youth-theatre productions, but it never occurred to me to put the two together. My mother took me to see plays and ballet and even once, recklessly, an opera, and I was enchanted and bemused in equal measure by what I saw on the stage and left it right there where it was.

At university I chose plays over novels whenever I could, not because I cared more about theatre but because plays were shorter and I could get three read in a week and still manage to sleep, unlike my foolish counterparts who took on the German novel and could be seen around college staggering bleary-eyed under the weight of eight hundred pages of Thomas Mann. I walked around with slim volumes in my bag and the words of Brecht and Kleist and Schiller and Weiss and Jelinek in my head. I acted in a number of gentle farces and even directed some Shakespeare. When I graduated, my choice seemed clear – I wanted to work in film. I returned to my roots, took a job at the Edinburgh Film Festival (I say job – I mean unpaid, CV-boosting opportunity), and fell in love with a man who loved film more than anything else in life, including me.

In those days, the Film Festival ran at the same time as the International Festival, and one night I found myself straying across the road from the cinema towards the Lyceum Theatre. They were advertising a play called *The Wonderful World of Dissocia*, and the poster suggested to me that the play was some kind of anarchic

romp involving go-karts. I remember standing in front of the
theatre and thinking, I have no idea what this play is about, I have
no idea if it's any good, I should probably be in the cinema, and it's
probably sold out anyway. But I went in to the box office and got
two of the last tickets, right at the end of a row in the stalls. I called
my film-loving boyfriend and invited him to come along. There
was a silence on the other end of the line.

– What's it about?

– I don't know. I think it's something to do with madness.

– Right.

– It says in the brochure that it's good.

– Mmmm.

Somehow I convinced him to come with me, and so we found
ourselves sitting in a brightly lit room with a glittering chandelier
above our heads rather than the dark space and the flickering pro-
jector we were used to. The lights dimmed and a woman appeared
on stage, tuning a guitar until the string snapped. She seemed
troubled. Then a strange man came calling. He explained the
cause of her troubles – she had lost an hour of time and had to go
to a land called Dissocia to get it back. (He also asked for a glass of
urine, but that's another story.) The play swept me into this land,
which was full of disturbing lift-operating systems and insecurity
guards and sexually deviant goats. I was utterly transfixed. There
was no Steadicam, no CGI, no fancy editing. Sure, there were
sound effects and lights and a lot of really ugly carpet, but the
world of Dissocia was primarily created by the human beings who
were inhabiting the same space as me that night. That world was
made by actors. And it blew me away.

I knew what theatre was. I'd done it at uni. But this was not that
kind of theatre. This was life. This was the impossible made possible. The play takes the most private, unknowable experience –
that of another person's mind – and renders it open, public, know-
able. It was incredible to me to witness that. I sat and marvelled at
the inventiveness and the wit and the intelligence of it all.

And then a small trapdoor opened up in the sea of carpet and a polar bear emerged from a pool of dry ice and sang us a song, before disappearing as smoothly as he'd appeared.

At the interval I asked my boyfriend what he thought. It's amazing, he said, it's really amazing. We ate ice cream before returning to that room to have our senses battered in a totally different way. When I left the Lyceum that night, I knew what theatre was. Theatre is a place where polar bears can come out of the floor and sing to you.

* * *

A few years after that experience, I wrote a short play based on a real-life murder of a young woman by an older man in Glasgow, in which I attempted to externalise the workings of the killer's mind. It was for a theatre series called Curtain Raisers, which were performed in theatre bars before the main show. My piece was due to be performed before *The Tempest*, but when the theatre management saw a run-through of it, they felt that the sexual violence of my piece made it an inappropriate curtain raiser for that show. It did not go on. I was angry, upset, a little pleased at having been banned. So it goes. A few months later the director called me to say that the theatre were now hosting the revival of a play by Anthony Neilson, called *The Wonderful World of Dissocia*, and management thought my short would work very well as a companion piece. What did I think?

Somewhere in my mind, a trapdoor opened and a little polar bear appeared. Congratulations, he whispered, and then he disappeared again.

One Day All This Will Come to Nothing (2005), *Cherry Blossom* (2008), *A Time to Reap* (2013, from Anna Wakulik)

Chris Hannan

I made my debut as a four-year-old. This was at Sacred Heart Primary School, Cumbernauld, where I took the non-speaking role of Christopher Robin in the school concert.

I was very much a Method actor as an infant. While my classmates sang 'Christopher Robin is saying his prayers', I knelt beside the bed and silently said some proper prayers; and when a big girl from Primary 7 lifted me into bed, in front of a packed house, I promptly fell asleep.

My first play as an audience member was 7:84's *The Cheviot, the Stag and the Black, Black Oil*, an agitprop piece about the history of the Highlands. I was sixteen. I wish I could say it overturned all my expectations of theatre, but firstly it was on the telly and secondly I had no expectations of theatre, never having seen any. But yes, it ripped through me like machine-gun fire.

I'm not from the Highlands, and, like the majority of Scottish Catholics, I regarded Scottish history as alien and abject. The songs I sang were Irish, and I knew more about the Easter Rising than Keir Hardie. The icons of Scottish culture, from Robert Burns to Rangers, were anathema to me. 'Burns and Scott,' Edwin Muir wrote, 'sham bards of a sham nation' – a phrase I often quoted with relish.

The Cheviot changed me. It was performed by Bill Paterson, Alex Norton and John Bett (among others), and theatrically it drew energy from the juxtaposition of stand-up, polemic, song and storytelling. It was staged (and filmed) in village halls, so there was a tremendous intimacy about the storytelling, and the subject matter was the clearance of the Highland glens by Highland aristocratic landowners to make way for sheep. I was watching alone, and I remember crying when a Gaelic lament was sung and then being annoyed/embarrassed when my mum popped her head in the door.

I can picture everything about that night – the pattern of the carpet we had and the plant that lived on top of the telly (in the 1970s plants grew out of telly sets) – because it was the night I became Scottish. Does that sound racist? Or nationalist? I expect it does – but on the whole I think it was healthier for me to identify with the people and history of the country where I was born and where I lived rather than continue in the semi-detached fantasy of an immigrant, conceptualising myself as a member of an Irish-descended minority living in exile abroad.

I realise nationalism gets a bad name – and I understand the reasons for that – but for me it's about self-knowledge: knowing the truth about yourself and your country. Anyhow, I'm grateful that, since my first play, theatre has given me several moments of illumination about myself; and I'm pretty sure that I continue to go because I unconsciously expect, and hope for, a machine-gun moment.

Elizabeth Gordon Quinn (1990, 2006), *The Evil Doers & The Baby* (1991), *Shining Souls* (1996, 2003), *The God of Soho* (2011)

Nancy Harris

My dad is the one who took me to the theatre growing up. A Cork man, from a family of storytellers and a writer himself, he dragged me to everything from am-dram to community theatre to professional stuff all through my childhood.

He had the least time for the highbrow, believing most of it to be stuffy and self-important; and this, coupled with his extremely low boredom threshold, meant that despite starting out with enthusiasm, we left most things at the interval. I remember one particularly speedy departure from a much-praised production of *Waiting for Godot*, where he said gruffly as we walked to the car, 'Forget it – he doesn't come' by way of explaining Act Two.

Given that I only saw half of most of what we went to during those years, I didn't exactly have that starry-eyed relationship with the theatre that people talk about. In fact, most of it felt like a bizarre boredom-endurance test that had little to do with me or the world or my place in it.

All that changed when I saw Miller's *The Crucible* for the first time when I was fifteen. Despite an old woman snoring loudly throughout, and my dad's insistence that I 'Wake her up!', I was utterly gripped. I wanted to stand up and stop it halfway through because the tension was unbearable. I was wrenched from the beginning, shattered by the end – I couldn't believe that something where people were dressed in seventeenth-century costumes and calling each other 'Goody' could shake me to the core and make me feel so helpless. But it did.

There were other plays that made an impact not long after – an obscene punk version of Berkoff's *Greek* that my history teacher sent us to by accident, *Juno and the Paycock* starring Rosaleen Linehan. But it was *The Crucible* that woke me (if not the old lady) to its power. It was the one that got me questioning and asking the question – how could I do that?

No Romance (2011), *Our New Girl* (2012), *Love in a Glass Jar* (2013)

Ella Hickson

My mum has taken me up to the Edinburgh Fringe every year since I was about thirteen. It was back when tickets were five or eight pounds, so you really could pack in ten shows in a day. I used to love it – we'd always start with *Shakespeare for Breakfast* and then rattle through anything and everything – some crackers, some stinkers. I remember some pretty hairy (so to speak) moments – the revelation of Elizabeth I as a transsexual was played no more than a metre away from my blushing thirteen-year-old face: my mum kept telling me to close my eyes.

The moment that I really remember was a performance of *Rat in the Skull*. I remember the theatre exactly. It was in a C venue space – black felt on the walls, and maybe thirty people in this tiny ad-hoc black box. I think it was in what is now the Carlton Hotel, I have a memory of tartan carpet. The play blew my mind. I was only a teenager, but I can still feel the strain in me as I focused, completely riveted for the whole thing. I'd seen some things at the National that had gripped me and the shiny lights in the West End theatres always excited me – but I think that was the first time I'd been, sort-of, mind-punched by theatre. I walked out and I *felt* different. I realised, I suppose, that theatre isn't just for watching, that it had power. I remember wanting to be part of that gang.

I said to my mum afterwards that I'd loved it and she said that I should go and tell the actor – and I did. I remember going up to him and being a bit bashful and saying, 'I thought you were great' – he was very nice about it – he said thanks. And just now –

writing this – is the first time I've ever googled it. There's a single review from the British Theatre Guide – the days before internet marketing. It was in 'Little C' apparently, by a group from Manchester University – the review agrees it was a five-star show. It was apparently in 1998 – which would have made me thirteen – it must have been the year of the transvestite Elizabeth: I saw a lot that year! And get this – the review says the following…

'It is impossible to fault this production. The audience is gripped from the start and the scenes between Nelson (Colm Gormley) and Roche (Benedict Cumberbatch) are almost painful in their intensity. This is a production not to be missed.'

I swear to you, I've only just discovered that in googling it. It could have been Mr Cumberbatch I said 'well done' to – mind you, could just have easily been Colm Gormley – if anyone knows either of them can you give them a buzz and see if they remember an impressed thirteen-year-old telling them they were great? And which ever one – well, in fact – both – could you thank them for inspiring me – it may have been a whole other career if they hadn't.

Eight (2009), *Precious Little Talent & Hot Mess* (2011), *Boys* (2012), *The Authorised Kate Bane* (2012)

Sam Holcroft

My first play, technically, was a pastoral scene in which my sister and I gathered paper artichokes into baskets for my parents' viewing pleasure. For reasons that I can't remember, I used to enjoy depicting the countryside in my family's London living room complete with paper-cut-out crops, and paper-cut-out fishes in rivers made of blue bed sheets. I don't remember there being any sense of narrative or character development to these scenes (and for this I have belatedly apologised to my parents) because at the time I was preoccupied with something else entirely. I think that gathering those artichokes into baskets was my first interrogation of the magic of theatre. This is not a real artichoke: it is a piece of paper. But a group of people, together in one place, are willing to accept, even if only for a moment and for the purposes of what they are about to share, that it is in fact an artichoke.

Ten years later, in 1999, I went on a school trip to the Donmar Warehouse to see David Leveaux's revival of Tom Stoppard's *The Real Thing*. I was mesmerised by Stephen Dillane as Henry and Jennifer Ehle as Annie. And again that same fascination spiked: I returned to school to write an essay on the layers of reality and pretence being muddled together as Dillane recited a fictional speech, while eating a real banana, sitting on a real sofa in a fictional living room. Through words aimed at one woman seated only three feet away, he was communicating subtle and complex emotions to an auditorium of a hundred and fifty people – and doing all of this while consuming an entire banana. Unsurprisingly this observation didn't score me many marks in my literary criticism essay. But my experience of that play, which shaped my experience of many plays that followed, was the wonder of a beautifully crafted pretence, which was so clever in its ability to make us accept it as real, even if only for a moment, that we stood up to applaud it at the end.

Cockroach (2008), *Pink* (2010), *While You Lie* (2010), *Dancing Bears* (2010), *Edgar & Annabel* (2011)

Robert Holman

I have always said I had not seen a play before I had a go at writing one when I was seventeen at school. Theatre critics who have interviewed me, even friends, have been lied to. The little fibs we tell can make our lives what they are as much as anything that is true, since it's easy to begin to believe them. In fact, I have vivid memories of going to the theatre twice long before I put pen to paper myself. My older brother Richard went to a Quaker school in Great Ayton near the farm in north Yorkshire I was brought up on, and I must have been about seven when I went to see the pupils in a play there. I remember it starting loudly with cracks of thunder, and there were lightning flashes as well, and sounds of waves crashing on a beach. In the middle of the storm were boys and girls with lanterns – it was night-time – shouting at one another. I had no idea what was going on or what it might be about, but to this small boy, sitting in the audience with his family, it was more than exciting. I don't know if the play was *The Tempest*, but over the years I've come to the conclusion that it was. The language was certainly double Dutch to me, and I didn't understand a word – I know this is true because I struggle to understand Shakespeare today. Did it matter one jot I didn't know what was going on? I don't think it did. It can't have done, because, as I sit writing at my desk more than fifty years later, the memory of my first time in a theatre, of a simple school stage in a cold hall one autumn, brings back an excitement that is almost as palpable today as it was then. I'm even wondering if I've told a lie about this in the decades since then in order to protect the memory and keep it to myself, to not have it altered by cold truth, to cherish it unblemished.

Then, a year or two later, came *Peter Pan* at Darlington Civic Theatre with Dawn Adams and Alastair Sim. I can remember their names and see their faces without thinking, yet to recall what I did a few months ago is sometimes a struggle. Peter and the Darling children flying about the nursery, even though I could see the wires lifting them up, made as big an impression on me as man walking on the moon a few years later. At home in my bedroom I tried to fly – my hands outstretched towards the window ready to soar through it – without the wires, and was disappointed when it didn't happen. I even wondered about rigging-up a system of pullies using string. I'm tempted to say I've been trying to fly ever since, and remain optimistic.

Next came a pause.

For someone who had not seen a play it might have been a challenge to write one, but ignorance is bliss. Mr Rudd, the teacher, said, 'I want you all to write a play during the Easter holidays.' The classroom was filled with discontented murmurs of how ridiculous it was, including ones from me, but, without having ever written anything apart from a few adolescent poems, I had decided I wanted to be a writer, and secretly I thought, yes, I'll have a go at that. I wrote it in an exercise book and called it *The Goldfish*, because it was about two teenage girls travelling to London on a bus and one of them had a goldfish in a bowl resting on her knees. They talked to each other and to the fish. I wrote it line by line, without any idea of what might happen next, and when I got to the last page of the exercise book I stopped. You have to understand I was not a bright boy, so to think I could write was more than wishful thinking. Mr Rudd had his favourites, boys bound for Oxford or Cambridge, and he met them socially out of school. A few days after I had given him the exercise book, I saw him waiting by the gate as we were all coming into school in the morning, and even from the distance I could see he was looking for someone. I was seventeen, and it was the first time a teacher had approached me. He said did I want to come to dinner on

Friday evening. A year after this he went to see my worried parents and told them I should go to London and write plays.

Quite a while ago, feeling depressed about everything I had written, I put the *The Goldfish* in the bin.

In my last year at school I read as many plays as I could find on the shelf at the library in Guisborough; it didn't matter what they were, and plays that Donald Rudd gave or loaned to me, which mattered more since he had a good eye for what was modern and interesting. I even read them in history lessons, which Mr Gee tolerated because he knew I would fail the exam in any case. I suppose it was about this time, or shortly afterwards in London, I began to understand that being able to see a play in the mind's eye is as important as sitting in a theatre watching it. It was reading plays that gave me some idea of how to go about writing one properly. I wrote at a kitchen table in Camden Town, with a call girl living below, and one night bullets through the window. I went shopping for plays on Charing Cross Road and found them second-hand in Bloomsbury. I am no longer in Camden Town, but some of these plays and many more are still on my shelves, whilst others, because I am not getting any younger, I have given away. History is the judge of whether a play is good or bad, and it seems right to me to pass them on.

Now I must finish this in order to have another go at writing a play myself.

The Amish Landscape (1992), *Bad Weather* (1998), *Making Noise Quietly* (1999, 2012), *Holes in the Skin* (2003), *Jonah and Otto* (2008)

Joel Horwood

I wrote my first play in my last year at university. Despite my dye-hard hippy parents' best efforts, I had grown up with a limited experience of theatre and drifted into an English Literature degree. The course was entirely uninspiring and horrifically traditional, so as an incredibly expensive and crap protest I had basically dropped out. At the start of my final year, however, I met one of those wonderful tutors. We read Burroughs and Orwell and discussed everything punk and possible in literature. It was around then that I had the idea for a satirical and stupid musical: *Mikey the Pikey*.

In debt, deeply depressed and with a crap Mohican that I'd shaved myself, I mumbled about it to a friend. I was really hoping that someone else would have the idea, put it on and that we could all go and watch it. To her endless credit she said, 'Why don't you just write it?' Before then I had thought plays just arrived perfectly formed. I thought they were conceived in moments of ecstatic genius and scrawled onto parchment like in *Shakespeare in Love*. Suddenly, it was possible to write them.

I sat down with a journalist's notebook and wrote a first draft in biro start to finish. I took a shower where I thought the interval should be. I had packed a kind of messiah-story structure with stupid jokes and bonkers ideas, but had done so with a very real desire to walk in the footsteps of those anarchic writers I had fallen in love with. Suddenly a script existed. Normally I'd write an essay about it at this point; an essay that I would hand in late whilst off my tits on Red Bull and bananas. Again, my friend (who we had ingeniously nicknamed

Goose 'like off *Top Gun*') said, 'Now you just need to put it on.' Again, this was mind-blowing. I thought productions of plays just happened when Mr and Mrs Theatre declared: 'This will go on in London's West End that the people should write essays about it.' Goose took me to join the University's 'Drama Soc' for £3. They mostly wore long coats and had clean hair whereas I had a fresh tattoo and had spray-painted my jacket. It was like they were Richard Gere and I was Julia Roberts. They were discussing the one production that the Gulbenkian Theatre would allow them to put on this year: Should it be *Equus* or *Endgame*? I suggested *Mikey the Pikey*. It was decided that there would be a Dram Soc vote. At the time I was playing for the university basketball team, so when eleven very tall men suddenly decided to join the Dram Soc and vote for *Mikey the Pikey*, I admit I had had something to do with it. Suddenly, I was directing my new musical. Which didn't have any music.

Growing up in Suffolk, I had learned to drive at the first opportunity (naturally I had also written off my first two cars). I used to give a goth friend of mine a lift to school, and he used to play tape cassettes of the music he had written. It was a bit like listening to the inside of Robert Smith's head, if Robert Smith had just eaten peyote and raw mince. He was the perfect choice as composer but had become a recluse. I instantly drove to Suffolk, way too fast and seldom indicating, and we wrote the music together over three days. He created some of the best, most cleverly pastiche music I've ever heard and then decided that he didn't want anything to do with the show because 'It was too much hassle' (code for 'Please don't make me leave my house').

When I returned to university I was told that there had been a backlash from the Dram Soc members who had not been present at the vote. The e-mail notification that their Gulbenkian slot would be used to put on 'a chav musical' had met with animosity. It was considered a 'crypto-fascist statement of endemic classism'. The Dram Soc president was deeply apologetic as he forwarded a message that read '*Mikey the Pikey* isn't big, isn't clever and it's certainly not drama' (a quote that we would later use as our log line). Seizing the opportunity for some reckless publicity, I swiftly

organised a march against *Mikey the Pikey*. My friends, the basketball team and a bunch of people with ill-advised haircuts
marched through my little university town chanting, flyering and
wearing badly screen-printed T-shirts stating our demand that
Mikey the Pikey be banned from production. The controversy led
to the show selling out almost immediately.

I employed Goose as 'choreographer' and a fella I'd seen being
funny in a band as MD. We held open auditions as if we were
X-Factor judges and cast not necessarily on the basis of talent but
on passion; we wanted people who were committed and brilliant
to be around. Inevitably our unlikely gang of misfits turned out to
be the best and most wonderful singers, dancers and actors we
could ever have hoped for. They fuelled the show with anarchy
and a beating heart. We became a genuine gang. But I still had no
idea what I was doing.

Luckily, my best friend had gotten into RADA. I would call him
every evening after rehearsals to ask, 'What am I supposed to do
next?' His replies ranged from actor's notes to informing me that
I would need something called 'a design'. I was lucky enough that
Ian Baird, a local legend figure, mucked in at this point and saved
me from my own shambolic ignorance. So too did a hoard of
friends from my past; Paul Calver took the publicity shots, Rob
Tucker designed the photos, Sam Simpson made incredible and
horrific prosthetic make-up, two mates that wanted to be stunt-
men began to create our 'gorilla advertising campaign'. Together
we made something utterly mental and completely satisfying. I am
indebted to all those who made it possible, to the actress who
secretly entered us into the NSDF (which I had never heard of),
and of course to Goose. My first play taught me precisely what I
wanted to do in my life. It taught me that I wanted to become part
of a community; that writing was something active, alive and possible; but most of all it taught me that I wanted to get better at it.

Food (2006, with Christopher Heimann), *Stoopud Fucken Animals* (2007),
I Caught Crabs in Walberswick (2008)

Stephen Jeffreys

In the summer of 1973 I broke from my usual practice and stayed down in Southampton for what was then called 'the long vac.' In the past I had headed back home to London to the Jeffreys family business (we made billiard tables) to pick up some badly needed cash.

I had no doubt that I was in trouble. I was halfway through an MPhil thesis on Modern British Drama. I had a theory which connected realism, Brechtian epic and the Theatre of the Absurd, all converging on the work of Edward Bond. But the theory wasn't getting anywhere. My tutor had ended the year by telling me that I didn't have an academic mind. Apparently I had a speculative mind. The summer was a hot one (although I remember wearing a moody black sweater for the duration) and the speculative mind was at work, though not on the most pressing problem of how I was to earn a living next year and for all the years that were to follow.

Instead the speculative mind was churning out some kind of synthesis between the aesthetic questions outlined above and the troubling state of the nation. Insurrection was just around the corner according to the newspaper sellers of the Socialist Labour League and Tariq Ali's new book *The Coming British Revolution*.

But in my mind, the moment had passed. True, the Tory government was cranking up for its confrontation with the miners which would see Ted Heath out of office in February. My hunch, however, was that we were in for a period of right-wing reaction.

1984 was not so far off. Supposing there were a near-fascist government? And supposing the long-delayed revolution happened then? And supposing it occurred, as in Cuba, with five people turning up in a boat? Where could that happen? Well, maybe Cornwall where the previous year I had directed our troupe in Arthur Kopit's *Indians* at the Minack Theatre.

I realised I was writing a play.

This play would somehow validate my theory in a way that the thesis never would: realistically observed people in a Brechtian framework but with flashes of irrational, absurdist images – what I would later hear John Godber call 'weird stuff'.

I drew up a grid of scenes, events and characters. All I had to do was fill it in, bit by bit, day by day, like Painting by Numbers.

I started writing. It was thin. It creaked. There were gaps. Maybe if I kept going it would get better. It didn't. I stopped.

I was aware of course that many other bearded figures had paced the corridors of the Student Union giving it large about the play they were writing. I did not wish to be part of that culture of interesting failure. But as October arrived with a new wave of freshers, Interesting Failure was the name of my station.

So I devised a simple strategy: I announced that I *had* written a play. I would book a venue and put up posters. In order to safeguard the secret that the play was little more than a mirage, I said I would direct it myself. I nicked a title from a poem by the revolutionary author Rudyard Kipling.

I typed out the few scenes that actually existed making three carbon copies of each page and called auditions. In terms of assessing the suitability of actors for the roles, these evenings were a waste of time as I could only focus on the grinding banality of the dialogue. So I plumped for a combination of old mates who would support me and new recruits who would be eager for anything. I seized on the cancellation of the sailing club's disco, and bagged a two-night slot in the Union Ballroom for the middle of November. Rehearsals were set for Monday.

That Sunday evening, with the die cast, I sat down to tackle the scene between the two oldest characters in the play. Amazingly, something happened. I didn't know what was coming up, but my pen kept moving with an inspired certainty. My hand seemed to be ahead of my mind, and with each exchange of dialogue the characters probed deeper and revealed themselves more clearly. And then the hand stopped. One character left, his purpose defeated. The other remained, sunk into his disillusionment. It was a scene. It was playwriting.

But now there was a new problem: I needed fifteen copies of a script which would run to sixty pages. Nine hundred sheets of photocopying would cost me most of my term's grant. The only alternative was the duplicating machine. I forked out for seventy waxed stencils and a bottle of nail varnish (for correcting mistakes) and set to work, starting at the beginning of the play, incorporating all the written scenes in the correct order, filling in the gaps and, finally, plunging into the great unknown – the ending.

The flaw in my plan became apparent immediately. Typing straight onto stencils means that the sharp type element misses the ribbon and cuts a letter-shaped hole in the waxy surface through which the ink eventually pours. But you can't actually read what you've just typed: it's just a hole. This was playwriting as an act of faith. After a week of hammering away, my cast, desperate for lines, helped me wrap the stencils round the ink-filled drum, feed in the paper and crank the handle. It took us most of the day, but by four o'clock there was a pile of fifteen crisp new scripts. I had written a play.

The ballroom was an excellent spot for a disco, but its obtrusive pillars meant that the sightlines were awful. The only way, I decided, was to sit the audience on the floor in the round and cover the floor in sawdust. Then it would look a bit like a Cornish beach and a bit like a circus. The circus was and remains the great sustaining metaphor of student theatre, so the cast immediately felt at home.

On opening night it became clear to me after a few minutes that I would be unable to watch. There was simply too much at stake. I found I could lie on my back on the floor behind the ring of the seated audience and stare up at the complicated polystyrene patterns on the ceiling. In this way the time passed more or less painlessly. The actors found my notes after the first show less than helpful.

Halfway through the second and final performance, I summoned up some courage and watched. To my amazement it was actually working. The characters were recognisable, but they were possessed of an oddly charged poeticism as well. The audience were drawn in. I had somehow created what the speculative mind had imagined: theatre which was simultaneously political narrative and metaphor.

I was astounded to see the university's intellectual champion, the Professor of Philosophy Tony Manser, amongst the audience. 'I've been here for twenty-five years and this is the first time a student has written a play.' He was generous and helpful. The play failed in its immediate objective: it was not selected for the final of the National Student Drama Festival. But it taught me one thing: I could do it.

Valued Friends (1990), *A Going Concern* (1993), *The Libertine* (1994), *The Clink* (1999), *I Just Stopped By to See the Man* (2000), *The Convict's Opera* (2008)

Fin Kennedy

My first plays were ones I acted in. I didn't grow up living close to any theatres, so these early experiences were from the inside out, performing two or three plays a year in youth theatres. Looking back, this is actually excellent training for a writer, but I certainly didn't plan it that way.

I was a confident child and that translated into an ease on stage. Early appearances earning my stripes as Second Villager in various Tolkienesque allegories quickly led onto larger roles as pompous Victorian fathers in drawing-room farces, or preening bullies in moralising teenage-gang stories. I honestly can't recall the names of these plays, though I do remember our enthusiastic youth-theatre director called Sarah, who had been at RADA but now taught Drama at a local school. Perhaps she had been writing the plays herself? I never found out.

Sarah liked to tell us she had been friends with Kenneth Branagh during her RADA days. Her claim to fame was having pulled him out of a hedge one night while drunk. She had a sparky passion and sense of mischief about her, which I loved.

Bugsy Malone was the first play I remember really clearly. I played the part of Fat Sam, and was able to bring genuine puppy fat to the role, as well as a cast-iron American accent learned from watching endless re-runs of *The A-Team*. We got to squirt shaving foam out of specially made Tommy guns. I loved every minute of it.

My parents were going through a messy divorce around this time. I later found out their marriage had been on the rocks for years.

Eventually, Dad met someone else. As the eldest, I was suddenly the man of the house, which included emotional support to my destroyed mother. Rehearsals were a welcome escape.

I quickly decided that I wanted to act. I have no idea where this came from. Perhaps from my mother, who, as a working-class girl in London's East End had always dreamed of a stage career. She applied to Rose Bruford College in the 1960s, and even had an interview with the college's grand, eponymous principal herself. Mum was put on a waiting list for a place, which in those headstrong days she took as a rejection, and went off to study Social Sciences at Hull instead. That decided the course of her life, and of mine. Mum ended up a social worker. If she hadn't, she would never have met my father, and I would never have been born. I still sometimes raise a glass to Rose Bruford for that. (I don't know if Mum does.)

I don't recall Mum ever putting pressure on me to act. I do recall my dad putting pressure on me *not* to. At his new house in Cardiff, he once sat me down and gave me the third degree about how unstable and badly paid it all was. Mum was a free spirit but Dad wasn't. These things mattered. He was right of course, but at sixteen nothing was going to stop me.

To prove I was serious, I enrolled for A-level Performing Arts at the local college, and traded in my sleepy village youth theatre for a bigger, more serious one in a nearby city. You even had to audition. Continuing the American theme, I performed the speeches by the young Vietnam vet in Robert Patrick's *Kennedy's Children*. That was also the start of a burgeoning interest in plays with a political intent. It disappointed me a little that the new youth theatre's first production was to be *A Midsummer Night's Dream*, though I was happy to settle for the serious part of Demetrius, complete with soldier's uniform and scowl (though happily no American accent).

Around this time my father was diagnosed with cancer. It was serious. He was admitted to hospital within hours, bald within days, and skeletal within weeks. Visits to Cardiff to see him started to take chunks out of my rehearsal time. I only welcomed the escapism more when it came.

At college, under the tutelage of another kind and thoughtful mentor, David Lea, I began to develop an interest in Eugène Ionesco and theatre of the absurd. I wrote essays on *The Bald Prima Donna*, directed and performed in *The Lesson* and devoured *The Chairs* in one sitting. At college I felt alienated by the rugby boys and party girls, dancing away their youth while I nursed a sense of despair at the pointlessness and fragility of life. Ionesco's plays spoke to me in a way my peers never could.

Three days before *Dream* opened, we got the call from Dad's consultant. He had forty-eight hours left. My brother, sister and I were driven through the night to Cardiff to say our goodbyes.

The youth theatre re-cast Demetrius, but I told them I still wanted to do it. They checked and re-checked – Dad had died less than twenty-four hours ago – but I was adamant. I went from the hospital, to the car, to the theatre. For three blissful hours I could forget everything and become someone else. I was seventeen years old.

That experience killed acting for me. Up until then, it had been easy, even if in hindsight I probably hadn't been terribly good. But after Demetrius, I inexplicably began to get terrible stage fright. A-level Performing Arts became a nightmare; vomiting and uncontrollable shaking before each performance. I just couldn't do it any more.

So I started to write.

My first play was an Ionesco-inspired existential parable about an ethereal waiting room, which the characters realise too late is in fact life itself. When their mortuary trolleys are wheeled on, they protest, but to no avail. It was probably a dreadful piece of teen angst. I remember David Lea saying he thought it was a pity I had had a mid-life crisis at seventeen. But that mortuary trolley, and the sense of an urgent frustration with life's empty promises, made a reappearance years later in my best-known play, *How to Disappear Completely and Never Be Found.*

At eighteen, I set off to Australia for a self-destructive gap year of drink and drugs. But theatre somehow followed me. As luck would have it, my backpacker digs had a professional venue at the end of the street. To this day one of my greatest-ever theatre experiences took place there, seeing Theatre de Complicite's *The Three Lives of Lucie Cabrol*. Browsing the *Lucie Cabrol* playtext now makes me think of the eighteen-year-old me:

'It is not until her third life, her afterlife, that Lucie discovers the survival of something more than bare human existence – the survival of hope and love.'

Lucie Cabrol showed me something more – that theatre can not only describe our terrors, but transcend them.

Dad wasn't around to see my first professional production, which was also my first play published by Nick Hern Books, *Protection* at Soho Theatre in 2003. But I am sure he would have recognised it. It was about a team of child-protection social workers in south London, and their attempts to heal damaged lives while nursing their own wounds.

I sometimes wonder what my father would have made of my theatre career. In one respect, he got his own way – I didn't become an actor. It's hard to say what impact his death had on my journey towards playwriting, though it certainly came at a formative time. One thing it did do, was cause me to search harder for answers to some fundamental questions about life. Drama is where I looked, and where I continue to look.

Inevitably, I tend to find more questions than answers. But every now and then, a moment of glittering and profound truth presents itself, and that raw, visceral thrill takes me right back to those early youth-theatre shows, where theatre was more exciting, beautiful and true than life itself.

If Dad is up there somewhere, I like to think he would approve.

Protection (2003), *How to Disappear Completely and Never Be Found* (2007), *The Urban Girl's Guide to Camping, and other plays* (2010)

Deirdre Kinahan

I wanted to be an actress apparently from the time I could string a sentence together, so my very very first play was written, produced, directed and performed by yours truly in my very own garage. My mother served orange segments sprinkled with sugar, and my best friend dressed up in her communion dress and sang the Our Father at half-time... a thrilling afternoon by all accounts for one group of unsuspecting kids in suburban Dublin.

My passion for all things theatrical, however, never waned, and I found myself once again in the hotseat as writer in 1999 when working with a group of amazing women at Ruhama Women's Project in Dublin.

I had returned from far-flung travels in 1997 and set up a theatre company with another friend (not the one in the communion dress), where we produced great plays at a blistering pace with nothing at our backs but a denim jacket and that feeling that you owned the world.

We supported our professional acting careers at Tall Tales Theatre Company by moonlighting as drama facilitators. And so one morning whilst hosting a theatre workshop at Ruhama, one of the women came up with the idea that we create a play about their lives.

The women of Ruhama worked as prostitutes in Dublin and were some of the most courageous, generous and wonderful women I have ever encountered. They also blew apart any notion one might have of the archetypal prostitute; their stories, personalities and circumstances being so incredibly diverse. The idea appealed to the entire group, and I – as always was and is my wont – was up for it! But as an actress, of course.

The ladies, however, had other ideas; it was their contention that we knew each other, we trusted each other, and I therefore would write the play. The fact that I was clueless was irrelevent. And so *Be Carna* ('women of the flesh') and Deirdre Kinahan the playwright were born.

Be Carna was essentially a set of five interlocking monologues exploring how prostitution impacted on the lives of a group of Dublin women. It wasn't at all voyeuristice but focused on their lives as Mother, Sister, Daughter, Wife, Friend and Lover. None of the stories were based on any one woman but represented a tapestry of experience, joy and tragedy as I encountered it in my work with Ruhama. We opened the play at Andrew's Lane Studio in Dublin 1999 and were hugely supported by the organisation and the women. We then toured to a number of small venues around Ireland and on to the Edinburgh Festival Fringe with a budget of about £2,000 (as you do at the time when difficulties are never difficulties and blind belief just seems to push you through).

I almost missed my own wedding as it happens because one of the actresses fell ill and I had to step into her role for the last weekend. I flew back from Edinburgh to Dublin on a Sunday morning and then off to France that afternoon with my amazingly patient boyfriend and increasingly frantic parents to get married the next day.

Needless to say, the wedding went off marvellously and I continue to try the patience of all around me with my passion for plays and playwriting and touring and all that goes with it.

I honestly had no ambition to write prior to that play, but the experience was so humbling, so thrilling and such an enlightenment that it gave me the confidence to have another go… and another… and another…

Moment (2011), *Halcyon Days* (2012), *Salad Day* (2013)

Dawn King

I'm seven or eight years old. I'm wearing a robe made out of a sheet and a tinsel halo. My wings, which are cardboard and silver paper, are magnificent. There is a power cut. The small plastic Jesus is welcomed into the world by candlelight. It's the first 'play' that I can remember, and it's magical. When an enterprising teacher decides to take the school play beyond the traditional bible story and also introduces auditions, I win the role of Babushka away from the principal girl bully who made my life miserable. It's a small triumph, an affirmation of sorts.

A few years later, I am a member of Fagin's gang in a local amateur production of *Oliver!* Nobody at school believes that I am 'in a play', but for a while at least I don't care about them. I know that I'm part of a gang. My gang steal sausages from Fagin's frying pan. My gang are bringing an imaginary world to life and going there to tell stories. I might not know it yet, but I have found somewhere I belong.

I'm seventeen and I'm about to experience the rush of first love. I'd studied Shakespeare at school before. *Romeo and Juliet* was certainly beautiful, *Much Ado About Nothing* was amusing, but *Hamlet* is something else entirely. Hamlet is full of angst. He wears black. He wants to die. My god, he's just like me. I love Hamlet. The play, the character. It astounds me that a fictional person can feel so real.

A run of firsts follows. My first readings of plays by Chekhov, Brecht, Caryl Churchill. They knock my head off. The first play I write is a the ten-minute piece for my Theatre A level. It's an angsty piece about a girl who is literally split into four different selves, which compete for control of her. The set includes an enormous canvas backdrop five metres square. My steadfast mum paints it in the garage, the only part of our house big enough to hold it. I'm part of a gang again. This time, the world we're bringing to life, the story we are telling, came out of my brain. I feel exposed. My heart hammers so hard when the lights go down for my play to begin that I might die. It's the best feeling.

I'm twenty-two years old. Theatre has slipped out of my life. I miss it. I'm unhappy. I decide to do something creative, to rekindle my early love by attending a workshop at Soho Theatre. From this workshop, Soho choose writers to attend their Young Writers' Programme. I'm not chosen, but by a lucky fluke, someone drops out and I'm bumped up and given their place. At first it's hard. I don't think I can do it. Then I start writing something. The characters begin to talk. The thing comes to life. It becomes the opening of my first full-length play, the terribly named *Arrival With Baggage*.

I join the writer's group at the Royal Court, and finish it there. *Arrival With Baggage* is given a rehearsed reading at the Royal Court Young Writers' Festival in 2001. It's a huge deal to receive such encouragement. It's enough to make me realise that I don't care about the career I had planned, or any of the things I would need to do to progress it. I'm going to have to be a writer.

Foxfinder (2011), *Ciphers* (2013)

Larry Kramer

I sat in my short pants at a makeshift card table in our front yard
on a lovely afternoon in spring in suburban Maryland and wrote
in longhand about baseball players. I hated baseball and I hated
my father (who called me a sissy) so I guess I was trying to please
him and I ran out of steam after but a few pages. I guess I was eight
or nine, maybe ten. The next 'first' play was a pageant I wrote for
the Cub Scouts about I can't even imagine what and remember
only that it was a hit, particularly with my mother who said something to the tune of, 'I didn't know you could write, dear.' I was
however old Cub Scouts are, twelve maybe. My first real 'first play'
was something called *Sissies' Scrapbook*, which I wrote when I was
in my early thirties (after my *Women in Love* film adaptation),
serious stuff, following four Yale roommates through the years. It
was done in a workshop at the old and first Playwrights Horizons,
where it seemed to go down very well (people actually cried,
which is what I wanted, and I fully remember the power of that
feeling: I wrote something that made people cry). However, upon
its transfer to off-Broadway under the title of *Four Friends*, Clive
Barnes of *The New York Times* wrote, 'With friends like these you
don't need enemies,' and we closed on opening night. So wounded
did I allow myself to be that I didn't write another play for many
many years. I was to learn much later that Barnes not only arrived
a half-hour late but was drunk, now a matter of public record.
Imagine that: the chief drama critic of *The New York Times* was a
drunk. I wonder how many other playwrights never wrote another
play because of this. Now I look back and see how much time I

wasted, that the playwright who just won a Tony at age seventy-seven had many more plays within him that he should have written had he not been such a sissy.

The Normal Heart (1993, 2011), *The Destiny of Me* (1993)

Elizabeth Kuti

My first play was called *The Three Ghastly Deeds* and it was written and performed with my friends Ruth, Lotte and Sarah when we were about ten. We stole the idea of a school for witches from Jill Murphy's *Worst Witch* books (this was, of course, aeons back in the misty pre-Harry Potter era of 1979), and then invented our own plot. The play centred on three witch-pupils who compete to carry out the ghastliest deed possible for a Hallowe'en contest. We each chose a character and got a chunk of the play to write by ourselves. My character was called Duncenia and she was none too bright but offered comic relief by misunderstanding things (an oldie but goodie). We didn't talk to the boys in our class at that stage of our lives – they were the enemy – so the play was entirely made up of female characters, and we were allowed to rehearse it and then stage it in front of the entire school. It was such a massive and uproarious success – in my memory, at least – that we decided to write another play the next summer, in the term that was to be our last at primary school.

This one was an even more ambitious idea – a period comedy set in the time of Queen Elizabeth I. It was called *The Regal Robbery*, and again it was a collaborative venture, each of us writing a section. My character this time was the villain, called Dastardly Egbert, and he was the one who carried out the regal robbery by stealing Queen Bess's crown. The entire school was trundled into the hall to watch it, and given that the school had about three hundred and fifty pupils it was definitely not the smallest audience that I have ever played to. We performed it on our very last day at that school, and so it became the swan song of our primary education. As we were leaving the playground for the very last time, one of our most lovely and enlightened teachers, Mr Strong, heaved open his classroom window and shouted after us, 'Your play was brilliant!'

Over the years Mr Strong's own writing has become very familiar to me – he is Jeremy Strong, the prolific and popular children's author, and his books now throng the shelves of bookshops and libraries – but in 1979 he was unpublished, and still trying out on us, the lucky kids in his classroom, lots of the funny stories he'd written (one of my particular favourites, I remember, was about a girl called 'Iona Banana' who got into terrible trouble whenever she introduced herself – 'yes, dear, you may well own a banana, but what is your *name*?'... and so forth). I didn't know that Mr Strong would be a famous writer one day, but I knew that I really cared what he thought of the play we had made because he was funny and creative and full of heart. His words of encouragement crowned a moment of true perfection. We turned and waved our gratitude – and left for ever.

I've continued making plays over the years – all more or less about ghastly deeds of one kind or another. But I will never forget the elation of those first two productions, nor the joy of hearing that shout from Mr Strong across the playground. I'm sure it's partly responsible – for better or worse – for the plays I've written since.

The Sugar Wife (2005), *The Six-Days World* (2007)

Jonathan Lichtenstein

Comedians, by Trevor Griffiths, directed by Richard Eyre, starring Jonathan Pryce and Bill Fraser transmitted on BBC Play for Today in 1979.

I was born in Wales and grew up in a small, isolated village surrounded by hills and rivers and air and bracken and didn't set foot inside a theatre during my childhood or during my early teenage years, so it is still something of a surprise to me that theatre is a large part of my life and that it provides me with my livelihood.

My childhood was spent in a kind of silence, refusing to cooperate with anyone, refusing to learn, refusing to read, refusing to obey teachers, refusing to listen to parents, refusing to smile, refusing food, refusing to get up, refusing to go to bed. Instead I chased small herds of bullocks over fields with sticks, swum with my dog in the Ithon, hid for hours in bracken higher than me, threw stones into rivers, walked in winter across the frozen lake whose ice creaked and called. In summer I swum underwater with fish, sat under trees in lightning storms watching the skies light up as rain trickled down the back of my neck. When the moon was out in winter I climbed hills at night and lay on the freezing earth staring at the sky and the clouds passing overhead, trying to read their messages as they made their way under the moon.

The consequence of my refusal to do anything at all was that I became a farm labourer. I felt the earth in my fingers, the scent of early mornings, the wind through my clothes. Later I worked in the North Sea, roughnecking on oil rigs, and it was during this time that I saw *Comedians* on Play for Today on TV and that I inexplicably started to cry and I hadn't, by then, cried for years.

What I had watched and which remains uncannily visible to me thirty-four years later was Jonathan Pryce as Gethin Price and Bill Fraser as Eddie Waters. It was just something I had never seen before. It's easy now perhaps to see why Gethin Price would echo with me then: a character unable to coherently articulate a social structure that he hates yet wants to be included in; a character who wants to erase himself but is incoherently bound up in himself; the inadequate, almost paralysing limits of verbal structures; the need to escape the prejudices of class and race and culture and sexuality that are constantly reiterated by the play's comic turns; the desire to transcend the ordinary world; the disgust at one's own collusion with the thing that one also wants to leave and destroy; the ambivalent warmth and exasperation between the father and the son. It is clear now to see the Dionysian Price attacking the Apollonian comedy circuit, the Bakhtinian world turned upside-down, the Aristophanes-like pleasure in disruption. But then I knew none of these things, as I couldn't think them or speak them. All I could do was sit stuck to a ten-inch black-and-white TV in a trance, not understanding why I couldn't move as Gethin smashed the violin. Trevor Griffiths, Jonathan Pryce, Bill Fraser and Richard Eyre spoke to me when I couldn't speak to myself.

Soon after the airing of *Comedians* I went down to an evening class, not unlike the one Gethin Price was in, with its desks and chairs and chalk. I enrolled in what were then termed 'further education classes'. I took A levels and then a degree, and I started going to the theatre over and over again, so that the auditorium became a place of closeness to myself, and later I began to write plays.

One day in 2004 I had a play open in the Traverse Studio during the Edinburgh Festival. It was called *The Pull of Negative Gravity*. It was set on the hills I grew up in and dreamed on. Damaged characters fell in love in the rivers I swum in. Birds flew in it and characters lay in reverie on the hills and the sky I used to stare at spoke to them and tried to heal them. As I waited in the queue to go in to see the play, a quiet man suddenly appeared at my side and slung something at me, a full carrier bag, which I nearly dropped. He said, 'These are yours' and then walked off, brusquely, swiftly, his head turned to the floor, one of his shoulders sloping towards the ground, gone. Slightly anxiously I opened the bag to see ten copies of my first published play. I had just met Nick Hern for the first time, twenty-five years after first meeting Gethin Price.

The Pull of Negative Gravity (2004), *Memory* (2006)

Liz Lochhead

My first contact with a playtext? This was a slim French's Acting Edition in 1956 or 1957 when I was about nine or ten and running her lines with my mother because she was in that year's 'Women's Guild Presents' evening of four one-act plays (three comedies and a drama) at the Church Hall. Though I could see that *Teenie Troon is on a Diet* – with Mum in the (leading, natch) role of the eponymous Teenie, a terrible snob with a Kelvinside accent ('and it's me thet hes to drink the watter the cebbidge is biled in') – was a play possibly, yes, more within the company's *range* than the 'sacred drama' entitled *The Road to Emmaus* with everybody in assorted dressing gowns & tea-towels & crepe-hair beards that approximately matched their perms but admittedly did cause some problems here and there muffling some folks' diction, nevertheless I actually preferred her Doubting Thomas. When wee fat Mrs-Miller-from-up-the-foundry as Matthew, Mark, Luke or John tripped over Simon Peter's sandals which had no business sticking out from under her footstool in the first place and went sprawling in a flounce of big salmon-pink bloomers elasticated at the knee as the Minister's Wife, the Producer buried her head in her hands, and the Session Clerk laughed, I can remember, although of course I could never have articulated it at the time, being earnestly and absolutely on the side of such bravery, transformation, imagination and risk. Why did French's only have cast-of-seven-or-more *females* plays all listed as *comedies*, anyway, while all the *dramas* were for six, seven, eight men with, oh, maybe one token female role, if you were lucky…?

The next French's playscript was *Oliver's Island* in first year at secondary. At our school every single form teacher, including those who taught Woodwork and Latin, not just the English teachers, all had to put on a play with their register class for the rest of the school on one afternoon and for the parents in the evening. Every year I would love this mad two weeks at the end of term when all normal lessons were suspended and you got to make the scenery in the Art class, might be called out of Double Maths for a rehearsal. In first year I had the obligatory orange greasepaint and carmine dot at the corner of the eyes for the one line, 'Oh, Oliver isn't it a *lovely* island' as Oliver's sidekick when to be honest I had coveted the role of the Cassowary.

After I saw the lad born to become Robbie Coltrane in *The Dumb Waiter* as produced by the Art School Drama Club in 1968 (Robbie and I were both '60s-skinny kids in the Department of Drawing and Painting at the Glasgow School of Art at the time) – anyway, after seeing him and *hearing that rhythm* I borrowed from every library, bought from every second-hand bookshop every single blue Methuen Pinter Play I could. Still have most of them, their pages long loose-leafed, arguably only adding to their lovely opacity and mystery.

There was the Glasgow Citizens' Theatre. Productions of *Galileo*, *Caucasian Chalk Circle,* oh, a wonderful *The Crucible* in a plain blond-wood fenced in set, *Waiting for Godot* in a circus ring, David Hayman in a *Hamlet* set in a mental hospital. Citz policy was in those years either all seats 50p, or Unemplyed and Students free, ensuring lively audiences, full houses. As I always wanted to read, and re-read, the play afterwards, more scripts to beg, borrow or steal.

There was moving to Bristol in 1972 and finding myself writing a rhyming play with an agitprop vibe about Anatolian Shepherds for my Turkish Marxist boyfriend to put on for the Womens' Institute in the Fry's Turkish Delight Factory in Somerset. Script of this effort thankfully not extant.

My own road to Damascus (not Emmaus) moment, though, has to be the first time I saw John Byrne's *The Slab Boys*. This was in

1978 and was a Traverse Theatre production in an unsalubrious former church hall for the Festival, a revival after the roaring success (you just couldn't get a ticket for that proverbial love nor) – after the absolute rave it had been earlier that season. It is set in 1957 and is about a (great, terrible) ordinary day, one winter Friday in the life of three working-class lads in a Paisley carpet factory where they 'work' in a paint-spattered dungeon in a non-job of such dreariness – grinding paint into powder and mixing it with gum arabic into samples for 'the designers' at their desks upstairs – that they have to make their own fun. Phil and Spanky, the hilarious, absolutely demotic, the then *shockingly* demotic, brilliant double-act patter-merchants basically torturing Hector the saftie, Proddy, mother's boy, not maliciously, just because it is really all they have to do, wanton boys, to get them through the day. A superb cruel comedy. As the best of them are. I have just re-read it – thank god they publish plays – and, yes, it is as good as I thought it was. I can still see the set designed by John Byrne himself, a complete Jackson Pollock of filthy jewel-coloured dribbles and splatters crowned by an only slightly maculate James Dean poster. I can see Lucille, the not-so-sweet seventeen-year-old universal object of desire, in her sharp '50s bandbox-fresh black-and-white striped shirt, her pasted-on pencil skirt, and patent stilettos, on one of her forays down from the office, hear her crack her gum as she lowered her eyelids to deliver another devastating put-down. *The Slab Boys* deals with art, American culture and sectarianism and class and aspiration and escape, the burning need to escape, in the Scotland of the 1950s. I recognised the big boys, and the girl, next door. The references are all local, specific, intimate and utterly confident, delivered with brio. And such language. So local. So specific. I remember laughing so much my face hurt. I remember thinking, 'Are you allowed to do that?' Well, clearly you were. And from that day on I wanted to try.

Quelques Fleurs (1998), *Perfect Days* (1999), *Medea* (2000, from Euripides), *Miseryguts & Tartuffe* (2002, from Molière), *Thebans* (2003, from Sophocles and Euripides), *Good Things* (2005), *Educating Agnes* (2008, from Molière), *Blood and Ice* (2009), *Dracula* (2009, adapted from Stoker), *Mary Queen of Scots Got Her Head Chopped Off* (2009), *Lochhead: Five Plays* (2012)

Linda McLean

My First Play was published in a collection called *Scotland Plays* in 1998. It was a thirty-two-minute play called *One Good Beating* and, because my surname begins with M, was nestled between Liz Lochhead's *Quelques Fleurs* and Iain Crichton Smith's *Lazybed*.

With the exception of the words, 'because my surname begins with M', everything about that first paragraph is so loaded with significance for me that, if I were David Foster Wallace, what follows would be two hundred pages of footnotes.[1] But I won't do that. Instead I'll rate the key words like this:

Published *****

Collection ***

Scotland ****

Plays *****

1998 **

Being listed on the cover, as I was, between Liz Lochhead and Iain Crichton Smith, defies rating. In my mind it still feels transcendental. Both of them were writers whose work I knew and loved, first as poets and then playwrights. Both of them were in textbooks I had read at school. Both of them had special gifts of the ear and eye. It's true to say I felt honoured.

---

1. Made you look.

With rear-view-mirror wisdom I would like to claim that the attention I went on to pay to the rhythm and metre of dialogue, observation of character and density of meaning, not to mention an ever increasing absurdity, was somehow heralded in that coincidental book-ending. However, as anyone who knows me will agree, the only real prediction contained in that first paragraph is related to the fact that the play was thirty-two minutes long and didn't fit easily into any theatre's programming, at that time. Safe to say that I have continued to write plays that are too short, too long, too small, too big, too violent, too lyrical, too...

...and so it goes on.

One Good Beating (1998), *Riddance* (1999), *Shimmer* (2004), *strangers, babies* (2007), *Any Given Day* (2010), *Sex & God* (2012), *What Love Is* (2012)

Conor McPherson

Nominally, my first play was written in 1989 when I was seventeen. It was a one-act play called *Taking Stock* and was written in the summer between my first and second years as a student at UCD. Two plays had called to me in the previous year: *Death of a Salesman* and *Glengarry Glen Ross*; *Salesman* with its righteous Miltonesque organ blast and *Glengarry* with all its swearing and jittery quasi-Socratic dialogues. Inspired, I wrote a play about some salesmen swearing at each other. Upon presenting it to the college drama society – expecting to come back in a few weeks and watch it being performed – I was asked, 'Who's going to direct it?' Not knowing anyone involved in the drama society, I realised I would have to do it myself. So I stuck an A4 page on the notice board saying 'Auditions' and that's what I've been doing ever since.

But the truth is we are always waiting to write our first play. Nothing we ever write can quite capture the pure vision of the moment of creation, and even our biggest hits somehow let us down. I suppose it's a form of madness. Recently Sebastian Barry said to me that Brian Friel told him that for a playwright to 'have a play' is everything. What 'having a play' means is that you have an idea you are thinking about, wondering about. You have a world whose chaos you can comprehend and even seek to control – a prism whereby the lunacy and violence of life is transformed into a beautiful poetic painting, full of motion and feeling. This is usually when you are at the note-taking, first-draft-scribbling point of departure. You feel that you 'have a play'. Ironically the closer you get to staging it, and an audience coming in the door, the more you wonder if you 'have a play' at all!

The Beatles had a running gag when they were starting to record a song: inevitably Ringo would pipe up with, 'You know – this could be the big one.' And Matisse always replied to the question 'What is your favourite painting?' with 'The one on my easel.' To have the privilege of being an artist, and the terror of always starting again, means that you are always waiting for your 'first' play. In this way the artist's life is infinite. And 'first' and 'last' mean nothing, whether you are alive or dead, because, in a strange way, it never begins.

This Lime Tree Bower (1996), *St Nicholas & The Weir* (1997), *I Went Down* (1997), *McPherson: Four Plays* (1999), *Dublin Carol* (2000), *The Weir* (2000), *Saltwater* (2001), *Port Authority* (2001), *The Actors* (2003), *Shining City* (2004), *McPherson Plays: Two* (2004), *The Seafarer* (2006), *The Veil* (2011), *McPherson Plays: Three* (2013), *The Night Alive* (2013)

Chloë Moss

There's a little patch of Kentish Town Road (opposite Pizza Express on the corner of Prince of Wales Road, to be exact) that, whenever I happen to walking past it, I get a little buzz. It's a teeny tiny fraction of how I felt when I stood there one summer's day in 2002 and picked up a call from Nina Lyndon at the Royal Court to tell me that my first play, *A Day in Dull Armour*, was to be produced in their Young Writers' Festival that autumn.

I'd written the play – about a young woman stuck in a job she hates, in a town she wants to escape – during the Court's ten-week writers' group led by Simon Stephens. I'd just about scraped the deadline for submissions and tried (and failed) not to think too much about it. That phone call happened during the lunch break (of a job I hated), and I spent the rest of the hour walking around the streets in no particular direction grinning inanely.

I remember thinking, naively, *I'm going to have a play on, if this is the only play of mine that ever gets produced then it doesn't really matter because I'll still have had a play on.* Of course it did matter, and very soon afterwards I got an agent, the brilliant Mel Kenyon, and a commission from the Bush, and then another, and now eleven years later I'm still doing it and can't imagine doing anything else. And even though I've had lots of great moments in my career since (as well as plenty of not-so-great ones), nothing has ever quite matched *that* phone call on Kentish Town Road.

How Love is Spelt (2004), *Christmas is Miles Away* (2005), *The Way Home* (2006), *This Wide Night* (2008), *Fatal Light* (2010), *The Gatekeeper* (2012)

Rona Munro

The first play I ever remember seeing was at my primary school in Aberdeen, Albyn School for Young Ladies no less. The sixth-year girls, who were of course demi-goddesses to my eight-year-old eyes, staged… something, I have no idea what it was, just that they were all dressed as gypsies and looking like gorgeous bandit/pirate kings/queens. I formed the intention to create theatre almost on the spot and proceeded to write a piece that I then directed, starred in and cajoled, bullied and harassed my classmates into rehearsing in the bike shed. We were all playing gypsies/pirates/bandits and had our mother's scarves tied round our heads. All that might have come to nothing had it not been for the help of a wonderful English and elocution teacher. (Can you imagine a primary school having an elocution teacher now? There was someone doing deportment as well, what went wrong? I've got an sh lisp, and I walk like a Shetland pony with bad feet.) This lovely teacher helped us move from the bike shed to the stage. The combination of live audience *and* adult encouragement was a heady, electrifying mix that I was never going to forget. I think the show was deeply flawed at a narrative level… I don't remember much more apart from the fact that I played a character called Pedro, but I remember feeling I had somehow failed the audience…

I didn't see any other live theatre of any kind, amateur or professional, until I was at secondary school, Mackie Academy Stonehaven, and I immersed myself in the drama club. Of course we were nearly all girls in the drama club so the first show I was in was a one-act am-dram staple called *The Six Wives of Calais* by Lawrence du Garde Peach. I played the butch wife of one of the heroic burghers of Calais who offered themselves up for slaughter to save the city from the English siege in 1347. I remember I *again* got to dress up as a boy (there is a theme here I have only just started to examine) and wear really cool boots and stamp about waving a sword as I was the butch one insisting Calais would never surrender and that we could slaughter the English. And then I had to see the error of my ways and realise this behaviour was very bad and break down and cry like the girliest girly-girl while one of the other sweet super-feminine characters lectured me on being a *bad* woman. I remember loathing that bit and dreading the crying. I was eleven.

When I was fifteen, encouraged again by several wonderful teachers, I wrote, directed and featured in a play that our drama group submitted as their entry into the community drama festival, up against such strong competition as the Drury Players. My epic was entitled *Lecture to Young Deities* (my toes are actually curling in retrospective embarrassment here) and was based on the premise that the world had been created by a bunch of student gods and goddesses left alone by their teacher in the celestial science class. I played the teacher who came on at the start and did a monologue about creating universes. I got my mum to buy me an extremely cool pair of boots for my goddess costume, which was seventies and contemporary. They were red. I wish I still had those boots. Unfortunately, the adjudicator, the judge who comes out at the end and awards marks to each group and says who is going into the next round, thought the play had in fact been written and directed by my drama teacher who I think he may have disliked. He also had a perfectly understandable horror of the amateur-drama equivalent of vanity publishing. So he went up on stage and *annihilated* my play, the text, the costumes (the boots! He had a go at the boots!), the dancing (and we were fifteen and thought we were extremely sexy, thank you very much) and the direction until I ran sobbing from the auditorium. In retrospect he did me a huge favour. To start out with the harshest review, delivered in public in front of family, friends and my whole community felt like the end of the world, but it didn't stop me writing, and, I suppose, if that didn't, nothing that came thereafter had a chance of doing so.

Saturday at the Commodore (1990), *The Maiden Stone* (1995), *Your Turn to Clean the Stair & Fugue* (1995), *The House of Bernarda Alba* (1999, from Lorca), *Iron* (2003), *Gilt* (2004, with Stephen Greenhorn and Isabel Wright), *Strawberries in January* (2006, from Evelyne de la Chenelière), *Mary Barton* (2006, adapted from Elizabeth Gaskell), *Long Time Dead* (2006), *The Indian Boy* (2006), *The Last Witch* (2009), *The Basement Flat* (2010), *Little Eagles* (2011), *Pandas* (2011), *The Astronaut's Chair* (2012)

Elaine Murphy

At age eleven, I went along to see my first play. My sister was play-ing a flower girl in the chorus of an all-female production of *My Fair Lady* at our local secondary school. As the fluorescent 'house' lighting was switched off and the warm stage lights came up, I was mesmerised by the power of the orchestra and suitably impressed when the ensemble appeared in full costume without a hint of school uniform. The stand-out performance of the night came from Professor Higgins: even though my plastic stackable school chair restricted my view so that I could only see stage left, I was completely in awe of his/her singing, dancing and the precision of his/her RP accent. (S)he received a standing ovation, a bouquet of flowers and for months afterward, everybody present delighted in the fact they had witnessed the performance that would launch that student to stardom.

After the show, my sister hurried outside to bask in the glory of her stage debut. We spoke at length about how she mutely begged passers-by to purchase her flowers, and I showered her with com-pliments on the intricacies of her dance routine, but the truth was I never saw a bit of her: she remained tucked out of sight on stage right.

Fast forward a few years, and I'm sitting in the Gaiety Theatre watching Martin McDonagh's play, *The Lonesome West*. I had tears in my eyes imagining the fate Coleman had bestowed on the poor dog and yet was splitting my sides laughing at the utter joy he took in inflicting such pain on his brother Valene. I knew

I wanted to write something myself, but every time a show blew me away, I pushed the thought further from my mind. I eventually found the courage after acting in two dire profit-share shows back to back. Since I usually found myself in the pub afterwards explaining to the handful of audience members (nearly all related to me) what the script really meant, I decided to give playwriting a go – I mean, how hard could it be? Quite hard, it turns out.

In my play *Little Gem* there are three female characters, roughly about twenty, forty and sixty years of age. By the time I'd finally finished the script, I was too old to play the twenty-year-old and too young for the other parts. For the first time I found myself on the other side of the table during the auditions. As proceedings unfolded, it became quite clear why I seemed to be more 'out' of work than 'in' as an actor: the talent parading in front of us was phenomenal. One of our last auditions of the day was for the part of Lorraine. In stormed the female Professor Higgins (a.k.a. Hilda Fay) from that very same secondary-school production of *My Fair Lady*. She delivered every line in a perfect inner-city accent and salsa danced like a full-blooded Latino, and even though there was no singing required, I knew she was capable – she was the quintessential triple threat. Needless to say she got the part. During the production family and neighbours marvelled at how I nabbed the now famous soap star for my fledgling play. Many boasted in the bar afterwards of their attendance during that three-day run back in the late '90s and knew, even then, she would go on to greater things. (They hoped my show would be another stepping stone to the aforementioned 'greater things'.)

My favourite play was a production of *Salome* directed by Steven Berkoff at the Gate Theatre, Dublin. For those couple of hours I was transported to a dream-like trance quite unlike anything I'd ever experienced before. Afterwards – as a paean to the cast – we drifted, in slow motion, all the way to the bus stop. If we are lucky, there will be a handful of shows that will amaze us, leaving us with an experience we are unable to replicate anywhere else. As theatre-makers all we can do is keep searching, and maybe one day we might recreate that experience for someone else – that is the power of a good play.

Little Gem (2009), *Ribbons* (2013), *Shush* (2013)

Joanna Murray-Smith

My father, a literary editor, bibliophile and historian, was a frustrated sailor, hence his voluntary position as President of the Australian Lighthouse Association. In 1971 he bought the family five berths on an ocean liner, to take us to England. I was eight years old. At each stop, my mind swelled with possibility. The world wasn't simply expanding, *I* was physically expanding it as I stood on the decks watching the vast white bow plunge onward through inky seas. We passed through the Panama Canal at night, the twinkling lights beckoning us through the darkness from a known ocean to an unknown one. In New York, I had my first glimpse of urban snow.

I had been surrounded by arty types from birth, and the world of the imagination was the world of daily life. Our huge bush garden outside of Melbourne was a stage composed of ti-tree curtains, through which the Australian light illuminated all kinds of dramas. The Olympic gold medallist Olga Fikotová fell in love with the American athlete Harold Connolly in our garden during the party my parents threw as hosts to the Czech Olympic team in 1956. The Czech secret service had watched from our verandah, fearing a defection might take place amongst the wattles and the fairy lights. Pete Seeger celebrated his birthday in the garden. Christina Stead and Dorothy Hewett, Xavier Herbert and William Golding sat amongst the eucalypts, and in summer I would lose myself in it, writing plays inside my head.

But when we arrived in Southampton, life became theatrical on a global scale. My father was a Nuffield scholar, and we had an apartment on Prince Albert Road. London was abuzz. While my beautiful, older sister made a bee-line for Biba, emerging weekly in cute beanies and embroidered folky dresses, I went to Primrose Hill Primary School, where I was astonished to learn French (unheard of in Australian primary schools) and observed that English children made do without catching grasshoppers at lunchtime. I was so appalled by the hot school lunches I had special dispensation to walk home, past the little church with the drunk on the bench for whom my father regularly supplied thermoses of tea.

My great-aunt died, and as a result my mother went to Harrods and bought me two new outfits in the chicest polyester and a pair of shiny brown knee-high boots, the obsessive observation of which caused my stomach to flip over with joy. At night I listened to the roars of the lions in Regent's Park.

My siblings had embedded themselves in groovy London. Occasionally they came to visit, bringing news of a city conquered by youth, to which my parents and I were largely and impressively excluded. In a rare missive from the real action, my brother burst through the door one evening clutching a copy of 'Bridge Over Troubled Water'. We stood around the portable record player, studying the spinning disc as we acknowledged that this was the soundtrack of the moment we were living.

One day that year I said to my mother: I'm going to be an actress, and she said: No, you're going to be a writer.

At home in Australia, the plays I watched were the ones in our house or in the summer holiday shack we had on an uninhabited island in Bass Strait. Ideas came packaged in the form of dialogue: passionate lefty voices rising over the penguins under the floorboards and the easterly gales whipping spray off the sea through the cracks in the sail-cloth lining the drift-wood structure.

As I lay in that island bed, I listened to those adult arguments eat up the night, and I felt the power shift from voice to voice.

Moment by moment, the voices carried a sense of indignity or outrage or injustice. Things seemed to be at stake, battles were being fought, language was the arsenal. I imagined what it might be like to operate the voices like a puppeteer, controlling the argument and shifting the balance from side to side.

But in London, the drama was in designated places: David Essex in *Godspell* at the Roundhouse, West End musicals, and my first proper play: *A Midsummer Night's Dream* in Regent's Park at night.

My mother had tutored me relentlessly that afternoon in Shakespeare's plot mechanics, when I would have preferred to read my *Tammy Annual*. But as I sat there on the grass watching Bottom wake and fairies emerge from the shadows, I felt the unmistakeable thrill of being lost in another's imagination.

What was this? How did it work? Unlike the paragraphs I silently followed as my father read me Henry Lawson short stories in bed at night, this story came to me in ramshackle, unpredictable 3D, a witty organised chaos, a wondrous human 'So there!' to the night sky.

Yes, I thought. I'd quite like to be the one who tells them what to say.

Honour (2003), *Bombshells* (2004), *The Female of the Species* (2008)

Bruce Norris

Well, what constitutes a *play*…? In kindergarten, at age five, I played a shepherd in a costume made out of bed sheets in the Christmas pageant at St Thomas Episcopal School – but that's not exactly what we mean by a *play*. A few years later I was to perform the small but crucial role of the bowlful of Jell-O (costume: red leotard and a washtub) in a lunchtime presentation at the Bendwood Elementary School's 'cafetorium' (combination cafeteria and auditorium) in an original piece of agitprop theatre written by our third-grade teacher, instructing us how to use the trash receptacles – once again, this fails to live up to our definition of a play. My first encounter with a real 'play' – a piece of so-called 'professional' theatre – was when I was probably ten years old. My parents were subscribers to the Alley Theatre in Houston (at the time, the only professional theatre in the fifth-largest city in the US – what does that tell you?) and, whenever they arrived home from a show, my mother – herself a frustrated artistic-type – would describe the *scenery* in elaborate detail. And, as at that time I dreamed of being a visual artist of some sort (I would later study scene design in college), I begged them to take me along some night so I could see all of this *scenery* for myself. So they dressed me up in a suit and tie and drove me downtown and we took our seats to see the play *Our Town* by Thornton Wilder… performed, of course, with no scenery. Damn.

The Pain and the Itch (2007), *Clybourne Park* (2010), *Purple Heart* (2013), *The Low Road* (2013)

Ronan O'Donnell

Does one begin these reflections by way of a veiled apology for the narrow ways of my experiences in theatre and the inevitable West-centric nature of my theatrical venerations? It couldn't be helped, even though, for me, the most influential play I never saw was Derek Walcott's *Dream on Monkey Mountain*.

I came from a home whose consumption of 'art' revolved around Irish rebel songs, the inchoate adventures of drunk uncles and other family myths, and the days I went to the People's Palace on Glasgow Green instead of to school. It was comics over books. The main source of 'drama' was the goggle box which, newly installed in 1970, sat atop the wardrobe in our one room and kitchen. I'd been taken to the panto on Nazareth House seasonal outings when I was very young and what sticks is not the shows but the glory and wonder of the auditorium, the odours of crowded foyers, bits of Fry's Chocolate Cream and bubble-gum sticky in the trouser pockets of memory still.

I was thirty years old before I again stepped across the threshold of a theatre. The foyer of the Citizens' Theatre spangled less than one hundred metres from the flats where mum lived. I'd hurry in and hurry out. The smell now of plush Axminster with various hints of red wine. The Citz was famous for its sets, and *Henry IV* by Pirandello was both sumptuous spectacle and brain food.

My first play was the year after Live Aid. I'd been downgraded from the open prison for putting a hoover through the visiting-room window, and as it turned out I was eventually reunited with the drama group in HMP Saughton. Andy Arnold, now at the Tron Theatre in Glasgow, was running the group, which met one evening a week, and the play we were doing was *Benny Lynch* (flyweight champion of the world, 1937) by Bill Bryden. I was Benny. Just after the start of the project I'd been promoted to the moorsecluded open jail and now was returned to the same group of would-be actors and a new Benny Lynch. He was a brilliant but flawed chessmaster sociopath, who in one rehearsal took a pair of scissors to the throat of a fellow thesp for standing on his lines. I soon got myself reinstated as Benny and remember persuading our despairing director not to cut Bryden's great play to a brief resumé. I could understand Andy's angst as half the class used the rehearsals to traffic drugs and were often too high to recall their lines. Somehow the mountain was climbed, and the play came together. Dim Dale was coaxed out of his stage stammer, the Darcy brothers didn't escape, and the hash-heids went abstemious for the last week of full-time rehearsals. Andy set the play in the round, in a boxing ring. The actresses were supplied by Stockbridge's Theatre Workshop, and on opening night many were the cat calls (etc.) when we did our romantic scenes. But gradually as the play progressed the jeering evaporated, and it ended in rapturous applause.

That evening when I returned to my cell I eventually, in a shy bigheaded way, got round to asking my cell mate what he thought of the play. John (he'd been a Marist Brother on the outside) after some thought replied that it became not me out there on stage and near the end when Benny was crawling through the snow he was saying to himself, 'Don't die, Benny, don't die.'

Years later when I wrote my first play and it was produced by the Traverse, there came a day during rehearsals when I realised what it was about and who I'd written it for. It was a conversation with a gallery of cons, my younger self and a dead man.

I saw *Uncle Vanya* performed by a Russian company shortly after I got out. I didn't need to understand the language to see and feel the translucence of the emotions conveyed. A glow of the hyperreal shared with other stunning plays such as Dominic Hill's production of Albee's perfect *The Goat, or Who is Sylvia?* When I bumped into Andy Arnold in Glasgow City of Culture 1990 (deep-fried Pavarotti sausages on the menus of the city's fish and chip shops), he offered me a job in his new promenade theatre company. I promptly dumped uni, and it was at the Arches, as a would-be actor, janitor and front-of-house manager, that I finally, irrevocably fell for the backstage and everything to do with the magic box of tricks that is the theatre.

Brazil (2004), *In the Bag* (2005, from Wang Xiaoli), *The Doll Tower* (2005), *Angels* (2012)

Mark O'Rowe

The first play I ever read was *Romeo and Juliet*. This was in secondary school, and the only thing I remember of the experience was noting that, in some versions of the text, Mercutio said, 'A pox of such antic, lisping, affecting phantasimes…', whereas in others it had been altered to 'A plague of' the same, presumably in case school kids would read something venereal (or sexually transmitted, as we now say) into 'pox' (or *do* we still say it?) and snigger every time it was uttered, which we did, of course, and which is probably the only reason I remembered it. There were plenty of other rude bits in the play, as I discovered many years later when I returned to it, but, since I had no memory of them, I believe now that our teacher either diverted our attention from them or else just skipped them altogether.

The first play I read simply for pleasure (well… the first I read for pleasure which blew me away) was *American Buffalo* by David Mamet. There was a lot of rude language in that one too, but the reason it made such an impression (to the extent where it made me consider writing plays myself) was more down to the fact that there seemed to be so much space and so few words on each page (compared to, say, a novel – another form that I was considering having a go at), and that a lot of those words were repeated, and that a lot of those words were 'pause'. At the time, the idea that a play was something which had to be taken from and added to and distilled and shaped through draft after draft after draft hadn't occurred to me. What had, though, was this: it didn't look like too much work. Of course, I later learned through experience that the effort required in making a play look that way was enormous and that I might have been better off choosing to become a novelist after all. But, again, all those pages and all those words, all bunched so tightly together, very few of which, in a novel, should be repeated, and very few of which should be 'pause', and for which I would have required great stamina and an extensive vocabulary, neither of which I've ever possessed, made me decide to stick with the original plan.

The first really successful play I wrote was called *Howie the Rookie*. It was also the first play I had published and the first I had produced in a foreign language. This was a German production, staged in Düsseldorf, which I saw on its opening night, and which was full of all the generous directorial 'assistance' and 'improvements' I've since learnt is given to plays in certain parts of the world. To be honest, I was in something of a state of shock afterwards. Even so, I congratulated everyone concerned (people seemed to have really enjoyed it!) and told them how much I loved their embellishments, persuading myself that lying through my teeth was a more philosophical course of action than giving an honest response. (What would that have been? Probably tears.) I remember, at one point in the evening, Nick Hern, who had also attended, being stared at by the director in a pretty aggressive way, and when I asked someone afterward what had transpired between them, I was told that Nick had let his own issues with the show be known, wondering aloud why certain theatre-makers just had to 'take something perfectly effective apart and put it back together any old bloody way'. Anyway, despite that moment of tension, we all ended up having a lovely night. Though, secretly, I felt (and still do) very touched that the play's publisher had courage enough to decry its mistreatment, even if its author didn't.

From Both Hips & The Aspidistra Code (1999), *Howie the Rookie* (1999), *Made in China* (2001), *Terminus* (2011), *O'Rowe Plays: One* (2011)

Michael Pennington

The first play what I wrote featured me sitting cross-legged outside a teepee philosophising while my cousins handed me my props. Fortunately for Nick Hern, the script doesn't survive, and after sixty years my cousins have – just about – forgiven me.

I adored panto so much that I kept insisting I saw Nat Jackley and Arthur Askey on the bus on my way home after their matinee (when they were, of course, busy getting ready for their second house). At eleven, I was enraged at my parents' refusal to let me see Max Miller live at the Metropolitan in Edgware Road, just because the BBC was banning him at the time. I punished them by mounting *Coriolanus* (yes, *Coriolanus*) on my model theatre and thereby learned the value of pace – that there are some audiences you have such a tenuous hold on that you just have to get on with it.

I was so obsessed by Shakespeare at the Old Vic in the 1950s that there are pictures (under lock and key) taken in our garden of my rival performance as Falstaff, wearing wellington boots, a silk dressing gown and for some reason my mother's pillbox hat. I got my first good part at school, as Chaplain de Stogumber in *Saint Joan*, largely because I didn't mind playing old and crying. John Gielgud's mantle descended on me in the form of his tatty old magic cloak hired from Stratford, and it gently slid off me again as I laboured through my Prospero. Rather adventurously, I did Karel Capek's *R.U.R.* and, hot off the press, put on *The Dumb Waiter* in 1960. How terrible was the day after a school play; how weirdly intense it had all been, alive, musky and erotic in a way I didn't quite understand, and how grey the Monday.

But my Damascene moment was a play that's forgotten now. *The Connection* by Jack Gelber was a big hit in 1959 for the Living Theatre, already legendary for pioneering Brecht and Cocteau in New York and more or less defining off-Broadway. Edward Albee, Norman Mailer and Allen Ginsberg were huge fans. Ken Tynan raved about it; he said people kept coming back to it like a Moscow audience dropping into the Art Theatre from time to time to see how those three sisters were getting on.

It had come through to London in 1961 and been sturdily booed by its West End audience. Then it filtered down into rep and to students. I doubt if the reps wanted it, but at Cambridge – whose university I anyway regarded as my own personal rep – we jumped on it. We'd done Cocteau and Brecht and Henry Miller too, and got into tangles with the Lord Chamberlain, so we reckoned we were nearly as cool as the Living Theatre.

But this was something else. *The Connection* was an evening – shockingly for the time – given over to the apparently random ramblings of a group of New York junkies in an attic waiting for their connection to arrive with the magic bag. It was a big long wait in real time, with lengthy jazz improvisations; we had remarkable players like Lionel Grigson at Cambridge then. A couple of times somebody silently came on with a phonograph and played two minutes of Charlie Parker and then left again. The play was a little ahead of its time, and would have done better later in the freeform 1960s. I was thought fit to play the central role and honcho junkie Leach: Warren Finnerty had won an Obie for it. Me, I'd done *Salesman* and *Godot*, and, a Strasberg devotee, I was ready for the enigmatic Leach.

The play had a light dusting of Pirandello on it, opening with a film crew come to film not actors but the local junkies whom they'll pay in dope – they were there as the audience came in, glaring and hostile. I bought myself a cowboy shirt, as like Finnerty's as I could find: it still hangs like a piece of papyrus in my wardrobe. I sloped around Cambridge muttering like an addict on the loose; I barely washed. I regaled relative strangers in the Copper Kettle Café with Leach's stoned delight that man might be transparent, his shadow created by different shades of black. All Leach wants is 'that taste, that little taste'. He comes tottering on first cutting up a pineapple and wincing at a bad boil on his neck, so of course I developed (and was) a distinct pain in the neck myself. I came to understand how junkies self-fictionalise. The one thing I didn't do was the main(line) thing about Leach, but I learned how it was done. I re-read *On the Road* and thought of myself as a real gone cat – maybe Leach was a little like Dean Moriarty – and I was completely and unchallengeably hip for a month. We achieved a fainting a night when Leach, unable to get his 'flash', overdosed, his 'frail line of life and death swinging in a silent breeze'. Nobody shot up on the stage in those days.

The reviews thundered that the play was 'boring and unnecessary', but I was rather sternly commended for 'facing up for the first time at Cambridge to the full responsibilities of a serious part' – as if I already had a career worthy of retrospection. In very truth though, for the first time, I began to see what being an actor would involve – a completely alternative life generated from within yourself but based on people you really knew nothing about – and that I might not have made a mistake to choose it. I was in heaven, with my feet on the ground. Oddly, as I squeezed my boil, whinged and strapped my arm, I discovered the perverse dignity of the job. The local rag called it 'A Play We Could Do Without', but I'm not sure my twenty-year-old acting self could have done.

The English Shakespeare Company: The Story of 'The Wars of the Roses' (1990, with Michael Bogdanov), *Hamlet: A User's Guide* (1996), *Twelfth Night: A User's Guide* (2000), *A Midsummer Night's Dream: A User's Guide* (2005), *Chekhov's Three Sisters: Page to Stage* (2006), *Sweet William* (2012)

Mike Poulton

I wonder if my first piece of acting counted as a play. It barely counted as a piece of acting as I had no lines. I was persuaded, most unwillingly, to carry a casket of myrrh towards a manger in which lay the baby Jesus. Nobody explained why. I was given no direction. Nobody bothered to tell me that on the afternoon of the casket-carrying the school hall would be full of parents. Even at age five I was beginning to suspect that 'acting' was just another name for a sort of massive fraud. I didn't know what a fraud was but I had an unpleasant sensation I was going to be part of one. The casket didn't contain myrrh – it was half-full of Indonesian cigarettes, which smell of cloves. The baby Jesus in his manger – a wooden box which said 'Cyprus Oranges' – wasn't Our Lord – 'very God of very God, begotten not made, being of one substance with my Father' – he was in fact my golliwog, whom I guiltily loved at least as much as I loved the real Jesus. Mrs Williams taught us in Sunday school that I ought to love Jesus more than my golliwog, or my brother, or my father and mother. I was quite prepared to give it a try even though Jesus seemed reluctant to turn up and return any love on offer.

There had been one inconclusive rehearsal. On the day of the performance I had been instructed to bring Plain Jane – my cousin Barbara's doll – to stand in for Jesus, who was not expected to show up. But I had reasoned that as Jesus was a boy child, and as my golliwog was male and had the sort of benign smile Jesus would have had, had he put in an appearance, he was better casting than Plain Jane. When, in the school hall, I produced Golly from the bottom of the shopping basket in which I had also packed the Japanese costume I was going to wear, together with my father's wakizashi, a razor-sharp sword with an eighteen-inch blade – I had brought it along, without asking permission, in order to cut a bit of a dash – my teacher, Miss Clilverd, looked uncomfortable. But my mother, always good in a crisis, deftly concealed Golly in Jesus's white Christening shawl. Only his black hair was showing as he lay on the hay in his orange box. Nobody had told me my golliwog was black.

My father, who fought in the desert, said that Jesus was probably dark anyway – he certainly wasn't white. Then there was a rather terse conversation between my father and Major Nicholson the headmaster about whether Melchior – the wise man I was to present – would have been Japanese. Being Japanese in the '50s was, for reasons I didn't understand, likely to be considered offensive by some of the parents. My father stuck to his guns, insisting that the wise men came from the East, and there was nothing in the New Testament to say how far they had come. My father had spent a lot of time in Japan after the war, doing something secretive he wouldn't talk about, and he won the day. He outranked the headmaster, and he was in uniform and medals. Despite my mother's objections I was even allowed to wear the wakizashi, though made to promise that under no circumstances would I draw it.

In my Edo period silks, among the dog blankets, dressing-gown cords, and tea-towel headdresses in which the other children were unimaginatively kitted out, I considered myself the lead. Hilary Farrell, playing Mary, wooden as the milkmaid's stool upon which she sat, merely gawped and grinned at her parents, who gawped and grinned back at her. I sensed that whatever acting was, this was not it. Nor was she good with her props. In picking up the bundle from the orange box, in spite of strict instructions to the contrary, she failed to conceal the fact that Jesus was swaddled in a pair of red and white striped trousers and a yellow waistcoat.

Joseph – the loathsome Geoffrey Potter – had a song to sing: 'Sheep on the hill lay sleeping / Shepherds their watch were keeping / Out on the hill / Calm and still / Sing Noel, Noel, Noel!'

during which half the class – 'walk-ons' – were supposed to wander on in their tea towels clutching lambs. The lambs were gifts for the baby Jesus. I worried about those lambs. I asked Miss Clilverd how Mary and Joseph were going to get a flock of newborn lambs, separated from their mothers, back to Nazareth – particularly as they would have to go home via Egypt. She had no answer. My father had suggested that a roast leg of lamb would have been a more useful gift to Mary and Joseph. Miss Clilverd pretended not to hear. Geoffrey Potter was the worst singer in the class and everybody knew it. Why had he been cast as Joseph? If Joseph was a singing role was it not perverse of Miss Clilverd to even think of Geoffrey? Why, when there were so many children more suited to the role – some of us had excellent singing voices – were we passed over? What had Geoffrey done to get the part? What had been going on between Geoffrey and Miss Clilverd?

The acting began. Miss Abbot – my father called her 'the bovine and lovelorn,' for reasons I didn't understand – played the introduction to 'Sheep on the Hill' on the piano. Geoffrey grunted the first few words so softly that nobody could hear, then faded and conked out. The tea-towel brigade that had started to wander on, uncertain of themselves, began to retreat. Miss Clilverd, flustered, appeared on stage and shepherded them into position. Geoffrey, in tears of shame, tried to make a run for it but was grabbed by Miss Abbot and returned to his place near the orange box.

Next it was our turn – the wise men, or kings. The class began to sing 'We Three Kings', which even at the age of five struck me as a bit of a cop-out. Clive Sansom was first up as Caspar with his leather purse full of chocolate gold coins. He was competent enough – adequate – but I can't say he made much of an impact. Nothing he did really engaged the audience. Then the verse 'Frankincense to offer have I' started, which was the cue for Keith Massey playing Balthazar to go up. But he just yelled 'I'm not doing it!' dropped his frankincense – actually pomfret cakes – and he too made a run for it. This time Miss Abbot failed to catch him. Keith's was a hard act to follow because Miss Abbot stopped playing the piano, the class stopped singing, the audience started tittering, as Miss Clilverd, in tears, hurried out after Balthazar. But even at age five I knew the show must go on. In the circumstances I did the only thing I could think of to regain the attention of the audience. Drawing my father's wakizashi I roared one of the few phrases of Japanese I had learned, 'Joto mati kudasai!' – which I think means something like 'Just a minute if you please!' – and strode purposefully towards the stage with my clove-scented cigarettes.

Later on Miss Clilverd nervously asked if my parents had enjoyed the play, and I said my mother had not but my father had. As children often will, I reported word for word what he had said: 'The bovine and lovelorn Miss Abbott played competently enough, but all in all it had been an imperial cock-spouting.' Whatever that meant.

Don Carlos (2005, from Schiller), *The Canterbury Tales* (2005, adapted from Chaucer), *The Father* (2006, from Strindberg), *Rosmersholm* (2008, from Ibsen), *Wallenstein* (2009, from Schiller), *Morte D'Arthur* (2010, adapted from Thomas Malory), *Luise Miller* (2011, from Schiller), *Judgement Day* (2011, from Ibsen), *Wolf Hall & Bring Up the Bodies* (2013, adapted from Hilary Mantel)

Nina Raine

There have been many firsts in the theatre for me. And they are inextricably linked to the age at which they hit me: much as in Jaques' speech in *As You Like It*. 'And one man in his time plays many parts, / His acts being seven ages…'

I won't tell of seven ages, I'll tell of three, and here's the earliest. It was the first time I felt the electrifying possibility of audience participation. I was probably about nine, a schoolgirl, with 'shining morning face, creeping like snail unwillingly to school'. I was taken to a lavish pantomime in London. We lived in Oxford, so making an outing to the capital was alluring in itself. I was taken with my younger brother, Isaac (five years old). Isaac was very excited. He loved fairy stories, liked dressing up, had lots of opinions on clothes, usually preferring to dress as a girl, and would often run into a room wearing one of my nighties, deep in some private play of his own, murmuring '…And she ran and she *ran*…' *Cinderella* was one of his favourite stories. I dimly remember a huge, packed, hot theatre, lots of red velvet and gilt – and the glamour of the actors on stage. Even then I was aware of their charisma. Isaac sat next to me, rapt. Buttons was addressing us as he tried to fashion Cinderella a ballgown out of various improvised elements in the kitchen: a tea towel here, a mop there. He turned out and exhorted us to tell him how to improve her outfit. To my complete surprise, Isaac shouted from my side, confidently, perfectly audibly, in his piping, piercing voice, 'She needs a *belt*!' Even more to my surprise, this earned a huge laugh from the audience – and Buttons agreed, she needed a belt.

Isaac now works in fashion.

Next came the first time I felt the sexual promise of theatre. I was a teenager, at an all-girls' school. Boys still seemed a tantalisingly distant entity. We were taken on a scholarly coach trip to Stratford to see *King Lear*. It felt vividly illicit. The dusk falling as the coach neared Stratford. The dark town as we roamed around, shivering, in the time before curtain up, some of us risking a smoke. Then, in and around the theatre, gangs of the opposite sex, in the foyer, in the audience, in the aisles. Foreign uniforms, green and purple blazers, grey trousers with a sharp nylon crease, potent acne. All the hormones made the play extremely memorable. And the coach ride back, arriving long after midnight. Then, came the news: our school was paired with a local boys' school, Magdalen College, for a production of *The Duchess of Malfi*. I suffered from stage fright: but I was enlisted to do the boys' make-up. I'd only just started to learn how to do my own. There was one boy I was mad about. I will never forget putting on his foundation, the sponge catching slightly on his stubble. The play ran three nights. He didn't kiss me. But I saw, not for the last time, the sensuality that theatre generates around itself, both on stage – and off.

Lastly, towards the end of school, there was the first production to make me see how exciting the radical could be, and want to work in theatre myself. This was a production of *King Lear* directed by Max Stafford-Clark at the Royal Court Theatre. By the end of the play the chaos was epitomised vividly by a dynamic, war-torn *mise-en-scène* in which someone, unforgettably, ran across the stage with all their belongings in a shopping trolley. This image imprinted itself in my memory. It was before shopping trolleys had become a theatrical cliché. For the first time in my life I was aware of the shaping hand of the director. The production had a very long first act, which ended with the blinding of Gloucester. There was a brilliantly oppressive atmosphere, and I became aware of a far-away tremor, the ominous distant shake of thunder long before the arrival of the storm. Finally I realised what it was: the rumble of the tube trains running through Sloane Square below. I've seen many other plays since at the Royal Court and not heard the tubes because they didn't fit the play. It was an example of the coincidences that often give rise to the most powerful moments in theatre: the random element that can produce the most electrifying effect. So much of theatre is down to chance, finding the right thing by stumbling around. The right casting, the right piece of music at the right time, the right place to stand. You don't know it until you see it, but then, it's right. And it's theatre.

Rabbit (2006), *The Drunks* (2009, from Mikhail and Vyacheslav Durnenkov), *Tribes* (2010)

Lou Ramsden

My first play was a film. I mean I laid it out like a stage play, and I called it a stage play, and I sent it off to a theatre. But whenever I read through the dialogue and imagined it in my head, it played like a film – complete with a range of outdoor locations, quick jump-cuts, and montagey bits. It's not that I didn't know what theatre was. I grew up in Birmingham, and I'd seen loads of great shows at the Rep and the RSC. But as a teenager I was so soaked in film and TV that I struggled to picture a story any other way. Blissfully unaware, though, I sent it to the Royal Court, and they did a reading of it as part of one of their Young Writers' Festivals.

I wrote my first real stage play a year or so later. I still remember that sort of light-bulb moment when I realised that I should picture a *stage*, instead of a screen, and go from there (…perhaps that sounds painfully obvious, but clearly I was a theatrical-late-developer). I had another go, and wrote a couple more plays. One of them – a one-woman show I'd written for a friend at university, on the cheerful subject of death row – became my first proper Edinburgh Fringe production. I went up there for a month with a group of my best mates, lived in a student flat on the Royal Mile, ate a lot of fried stuff and Angel Delight, and loved the whole thing. Reviewers were quite nice to us, and one of them – who'd read or seen something I'd written earlier – called me a 'steadily maturing playwright'. I was quietly chuffed, until my friend Sean said it made me sound like a cheese.

The first new play to really knock my socks off was a few years later again. By then I'd done a Royal Court group with Simon Stephens, written two radio plays, and seen loads of shows I'd really enjoyed. But nothing changed my theatrical outlook quite like Paines Plough's first production of *Mercury Fur* by Philip Ridley at the Menier Chocolate Factory. It was wild, weird, grisly, and beautiful. And it showed me that I could do more than just picture a stage – I could use the circumstances of the theatre as well. The fact that the audience were in an inescapable black box served to ramp up the tension of the play, to unbearable levels. The pressure-cooker-plot boiled, and bubbled over. My heart literally pounded. I was thrilled by the revelation that theatre could be more than just an exercise in language, or a nice, polite, passively watched story – it could elicit a physical reaction, giving people a horrifyingly visceral roller-coaster ride. I felt sort of similar following *After the End* by Dennis Kelly at the Bush. Uncomfortable, tense, raw, emotional… but in a good way.

My first professional production was a coming-of-age story about a girl from a dogfighting family, *Breed*. It was born out of a newspaper story I read about a woman in her forties, a mother of two, who was sent down after a dogfighting 'party' she was running was infiltrated by police. Something about the subject matter drew me in, and I tried to instil the story with a little of the energy, pace, and tension I'd felt at *Mercury Fur*. The script isn't flawless, of course, but I'm still (weirdly) proud of the little gasps we got from the audience at Theatre503 on several nights, and the people who watched the last scene through their hands.

So I suppose, like many writers, my career so far has been a series of firsts, realisations and revelations – and I hope it carries on like that. I know the theatre I like right now, but I've got no doubt that'll change as I carry on… erm… steadily maturing. One of the most brilliant things about theatre – watching it and writing it – is the opportunity to discover new and surprising stuff all the time. I hope I carry on having Firsts for years to come.

Breed (2010), *Hundreds and Thousands* (2011)

Morna Regan

I got 50p and a new dress to be in *Shoo Fly Don't Bother Me* at primary school and thought it was a very lucrative deal altogether and so went on to become an actress. Little did I know I had actually peaked.

Another peak. The first play I ever saw was the world premiere of Brian Friel's *Translations* in the Guildhall in Derry. I was only twelve but that experience, in that time and place, went on to form me massively as an actor, a writer and an Irish woman. Decades later, it is still doing that.

Midden (2001), *The House Keeper* (2012)

Billy Roche

My father was an ex-professional boxer – a big, charismatic bruiser of a man with a broken nose and busted thumbs and the makings of a cauliflower ear. He had an interesting face which, on entering a room, would never fail to set it – and everyone in it – aglow (just think Cyrano de Bergerac with a Wexford accent). He was also a singer and musician and a bit of a light entertainer who, for such a strong man, was incredibly dainty on his feet. Therefore from time to time he would be asked to appear as MC or a special guest in various local amateur/variety shows.

The first play I can recall going to see had my father cast as… yes, a big bruiser with a broken nose and busted thumbs. It was called *The Whole Town's Talking*. Don't ask me who wrote it or what it was about because I was no more than six or seven at the time and I was only interested in one thing: the little fellow swinging from the chandelier in the final act.

For weeks beforehand my father would rehearse in our tiny kitchen, pacing up and down the room while my sister Brenda fed him his lines and prompted him whenever he ran out of words. 'Don't tell me,' he'd say. 'I know it… No, can't seem to…' and I'd envy her as she'd reluctantly stammer out in staccato the beginnings of the next line until he found his feet again. The highlight though was the last page – the swinging chandelier and my father falling dramatically to the floor.

I'm not so sure my mother approved of this acting lark. She certainly never got involved in the run-up anyway; in fact sometimes she seemed to be deliberately trying to sabotage the campaign – serving tea or calling out that *Twenty Questions* was on the radio. My father knew the score – namely that she was out to thwart him – and he kept his head well below the parapet. Even at my tender age I suspected that there was a leading lady in the frame that my mother was not too fond of. Although to be fair, when it came near time to see the show she had all our tickets bought and paid for without any hint of encouragement or reminder from any of us.

The play was taking place in the Theatre Royal. Our seats were up in the balcony. It was, needless to say, a bit of a novelty – the fancy sweets and the printed programme and the glint of the velvet drapes and the ushers and usherettes literally darting about as if everything was a do-or-die matter. And yes, I was in my element, although it wasn't my first time here by any means. I – an old hand – had seen at least two or three pantomimes by then, and the ghost of that thrill still had me enthralled: the songs and the dancing and the strange feeling I got whenever Robin Hood slapped his beautiful thighs; it was a gorgeous woman playing the part and although I actually knew her by name nevertheless he, or she, called herself Robin Hood and ran with the boys and fought like a man and sang love songs to Maid Marian, so... Confused? – I'll say!

But *The Whole Town's Talking* was different. This was a real stage play with no one singing or dancing, and my father had one of the starring roles. I knew from watching his private rehearsals that towards the end (which is all I can remember now) my father would burst onto the stage and accuse the little leading man of something or other (adultery more than likely), and, just when he was on the verge of clouting the little lad, the lights would suddenly dim, plunging us all into utter darkness and out-of-sight confusion. By the time the lights rose again, my father would be on the deck and the little fellow would be swinging from the overhead chandelier.

I would lie awake at night picturing this glittering chandelier and marvelling as the petite hero dangled from it on high, like Charlie Chaplin or Norman Wisdom. Sometimes he'd be upside-down, balanced precariously by the tips of his toes. Other times he'd be hanging on with one hand like a trapeze artist, or he might be using his two hands and yodelling like Tarzan. Either way it was going to be a sight to see. I told all my school chums about it and anyone else who'd listen, and I'd put money on it that my enthusiasm upped tickets sales no end.

And that would have been fine and dandy except it wasn't a sight to see. No, there was no chandelier. When the lights rose the little actor was not swinging from anything. He was sitting rather awkwardly, and foolishly, on top of a nearby sideboard which was wobbling beneath his weight, so much so that the whole auditorium issued a collective worried sound for his safety. And then the lights went down and I – bitterly disappointed and, I must admit, a little ashamed of my association with it all – hung my head in the dark.

My mother seemed pleased with the way the evening went, particularly when the woman behind her agreed that the leading lady's performance was not really up to scratch. My father got good reviews from all and sundry, however, and my mother was so gratified that she bought us chips and rissoles on the way home. No one mentioned the chandelier – or the lack of it – and I knew better than to bring it up. No, I just polished off my chips and sucked up the vinegar from the corner of the bag. It would be years later before I came to realise that *The Whole Town's Talking* had taught me a valuable writing lesson in theatrical economy that night: *forget the chandelier*.

A Handful of Stars (1989), *Poor Beast in the Rain* (1990), *The Wexford Trilogy* (1992, 2000), *The Cavalcaders & Amphibians* (1994), *On Such As We* (2002), *Lay Me Down Softly* (2008)

Tanya Ronder

The first play I remember was the circus in Edinburgh, I was five. The clowns took me from the audience and sat me on top of a tee-tering pile of chairs. I was captivated – scared, thrilled and totally alert. Theatre swam in to my world.

The first time I remember going to the theatre on my own as a young adult, was to see Sam Shepard's *Fool for Love* at the Lyric on Shaftesbury Avenue, starring Julie Walters and Ian Charleson. I was so mesmerised I walked straight back in to the foyer in a trance (I'd been sat in the gods), spent everything I had on the playscript and read it twice through, back-to-back.

Sitting quietly in the auditorium, after theatre visits that bypass cynicism and grumblings, is my favourite thing. Feeling the space resonant with the performance. When I wrote my first play, an adaptation of Lope de Vega's *Peribanez* for the Young Vic in 2003, I liked to sneak up to the balcony on my own and watch. The thrill of arriving at the theatre for the first preview, to a queue of people and the printed play, was as heady as being on that pile of chairs. Only I'd finally got out of the arena by giving up acting. I was so happy to be back with the audience.

Peribanez (2003, from de Vega), *Blood Wedding* (2005, from Lorca), *Vernon God Little* (2007, 2011, adapted from DBC Pierre), *Table* (2013)

Diane Samuels

In childbirth, there is a moment before the head of the baby 'crowns' when it feels utterly impossible to get the thing out.

'I can't.' I hollered, 'I can't do this. I can't can't can't!'

I meant it. I couldn't. I *really* meant it.

'Breathe.' The midwife was an old hand. 'Pant.'

No battle left in me. Surrender. What choice was there? So I gave up. The pushes had a life of their own, coming hard, harder, and then the biggest push bursting through any final speck of resistance. Head first, body soon after. Suddenly it was done. He was out.

As my first son lay on my belly, I said, 'If I can do that, I can do anything.'

This is how I started to write plays for a living.

At the time, I was Education Officer at the Unicorn Theatre for children, based at the Arts Theatre on Great Newport Street, a spit and a hop from Leicester Square tube station. I was responsible for writing, designing, printing, folding, stapling and lugging down the steep stairs the teachers' notes to accompany productions of the plays produced at the theatre for school and family audiences. I preferred this job to full-time teaching. I'd previously taught drama in inner London secondary schools, most notably at the infamous Hackney Downs, where Harold Pinter had once been a pupil in its grammar-school days. I landed there during its later comprehensive era when Thatcher's government

singled it out as a pernicious hotbed of radical education. I worked
with some remarkable colleagues, devoted educators, who taught
me how to go about inspiring personal evolution alongside a sense
of social responsibility. We were devoted to triggering political
change through learning, something that has always informed my
writing. But bearing with the timetables, the curriculum
requirements, the demands of class management, the sheer 9-to-
5-ness of it all, the enabling others all the time when I wished I
had the courage to pour out the stories and characters alive in me,
was proving less and less tenable. I had to find a way to bridge the
gulf between doing a job and making a career out of a creative life.
Somewhere in my deep programming, as is all too common in
this culture, was the message that art does not sustain a livelihood,
that 'playing' and 'stories' are no more than a childish pastime.
Then there was a deeper fear that the 'voices' I might express could
well reveal me to be at best a fool and most probably insane. How
does anyone begin to let out onto a page even a flicker of the inner
tangles, messy fantasies, raw passions that can so easily expose a
soul to unending shame? How easy, you warn yourself, it is to
write badly or self-indulgently. Too easy. Best avoid taking the risk.
Still, the classroom was wearing me down. So I'd leapt at the
chance after maternity leave to work for far less money at the
Unicorn in a sane and sensible education role. I was happy enough
being endlessly inventive with suggestions for activities to
accompany David Wood's irrepressible and ever-popular *Meg and
Mog*, an adaptation of Roald Dahl's *The Twits*, a wondrous and
batty one-man show by Ken Campbell, and Bernard Ashley's first
stage play. I watched the masters in action and wondered how.
Well practised in drama teaching and devising ensemble plays
though I was, I preferred hiding within the group and supporting
others to forge an authorial team. I hovered on the brink of
working out how to begin a script from scratch on the page, wary
as hell of standing alone and having to account for myself. After
conceiving the idea that I could do anything, I now found myself
suspended in the crowning moment of 'I can't I can't I can't...'

I was also in the midst of completing a part-time course for an
advanced diploma in Drama in Education at Central School for

Speech and Drama. This was run by the charismatic, endlessly provocative and non-conformist David Herbert. The course required for final assessment a substantial piece of original work from each participant. David mused that if we had nurtured a secret longing to act then we might decide to present a performance to an audience, or if we'd prefer to write an academic treatise on a director, play or playwright, that would be fine, or if we wanted to write our own play, perhaps…

I was knackered from disturbed nights and endless breastfeeding. I had got that bloody head out of me, but now I was struggling to keep up the everyday momentum.

Then David said the thing that gave me the final push.

'Choose to do something that you're afraid of doing, because what else is the point? This is your chance. Take it. Otherwise, when will you?'

So I surrendered to the urge, rode the fear and wrote *Whatever Happened to Janet and John?*, creating roles for two other women on the course who were both terrified of acting and were daring themselves to face a public audience. This one-act piece played with life story as fiction. A woman in her thirties must somehow free herself from the legacy of being cast as the model child in a set of early readers written and illustrated by her mother. There she is, captured in a pastel childhood, for all to learn to read by, and yet there she never was. A darker truth, of course, lies below the surface, because the brother with whom she is forever paired in literary idyll, died before the books were written. After sharing the play with fellow students, family and friends, I was encouraged to adapt it for radio and it went on to win a *Radio Times* prize, opening the door to my becoming a radio dramatist.

My eldest son is now in his mid-twenties and I look at this six-foot, bearded man, and wonder still, as I do when I see any of my plays in completed form, how on earth did I contribute to creating such a self-determining life.

Kindertransport (1995), *The True Life Fiction of Mata Hari* (2002), *3 Sisters on Hope Street* (2008, with Tracy-Ann Oberman)

Antony Sher

The first play that blew me away was Athol Fugard's *Hello and Goodbye*. I saw the original production in Cape Town in 1965. I was a schoolboy, aged sixteen.

At that time, the theatre in my hometown was not particularly distinguished. The open-air theatre at Maynardville did one Shakespeare production a year, aimed mainly for school parties, and performed in an old-fashioned style reminiscent of British Shakespeare in the '50s, a style sometimes described as 'starched vowels and wrinkly tights'. There was also a local rep company, CAPAB, churning out their versions of West End or Broadway fare, like *The Chalk Garden* and *Barefoot in the Park*. Our meagre theatre diet was one of the casualties (a minor one, it must be said) of apartheid. What with the government's Censorship Board banning any controversial material from entering the country, and the Cultural Boycott causing writers like Pinter and Wesker to withhold their work from South Africa – there wasn't much left.

Into this void stepped a young, unknown playwright from Port Elizabeth, Athol Fugard. I remember thinking what a strange name it was. But as my mother and I took our seats in the Little Theatre that evening in 1965 to see his play, *Hello and Goodbye*, things were about to get much stranger.

He was writing about poor whites, one of the most marginalised groups in our racially torn country. Yet here I was watching a play about them: a brother and sister having a reunion in the house where they were brought up. Hester is a prostitute, Johnnie is a recluse. (He was played by Fugard himself.) They meet, talk, fight, and part. That's it. The entire plot is in the title. But what amazed me is how real the characters seemed, how raw, and how their dialogue was a stew of everyday speech: curses and quips, advertising jingles, now a string of clichés, now spontaneous poetic images, and half-finished thoughts, exclamations, and grunts. I didn't know that people could talk like this in plays. But it wasn't only the sound of Fugard's writing – like a new kind of music – there was also the feel of it, the punch.

A moment in the second half hit me powerfully that night, and still seems very special. The siblings are unpacking suitcases of old family belongings, and find a woman's dress:

HESTER. My God, Johnnie! Smell!

JOHNNIE. What?

HESTER. It's her.

JOHNNIE. Who?

HESTER. Mommie. Smell, man. It's Mommie's smell.

Sitting next to my own mother, I felt tears come to my eyes. I didn't know plays could make you cry. I didn't know theatre could do that.

It was the use of that word, 'Mommie'. Poor whites might have seemed like an alien people to me, but 'Mommie' was what we Sher kids also called out in the dark. And Hester says, 'Aina!' – our customary cry of pain – and 'Hell, man!', one of my father's favourite expressions.

Hester and Johnnie were certainly more familiar to me than the reserved English governess in *The Chalk Garden*, the kooky American couple in *Barefoot in the Park*, or the hammy Shakespeare characters bestriding the grassy stage at Maynardville.

Fugard was holding up a mirror to nature, and, for me, it held a most unexpected revelation. South African people, South African stories – these were as valid in Drama as those from any other nation.

I didn't realise it till much later, but the director of that original production of *Hello and Goodbye* was Barney Simon, who would go on to co-found the Market Theatre in Joburg, and help to create a specific kind of South African theatre – Protest Theatre – which would do battle with the apartheid government, and astonish the world with its achievements, both politically and artistically. Fugard was at the forefront of that movement, of course, and in his collaborations with the actors John Kani and Winston Ntshona – *Siswe Banzi Is Dead* and *The Island* – they created two masterpieces of modern drama.

In 1981, sixteen years after seeing *Hello and Goodbye* , I finally met Fugard in London, and told him how important his play had been to me. It put reality and truth on stage, it swept away artificiality, it made theatre seem important – no, vital. He accepted my praise for the play, but not, oddly enough, for his performance as Johnnie, which I remembered as being equally remarkable – the way he played a simple man without patronising him. But although he was then about to play General Smuts in the film *Gandhi*, he did not regard himself as much of an actor.

Disbelieving him, yet also somehow liberated by the information, I now had the courage to try the part myself. In 1988, the RSC mounted a production at the Almeida Theatre, where I was joined by two formidable South African talents: the actress Estelle Kohler playing Hester, and the director Janice Honeyman. It was a tremendous experience: a defining moment from my youthful theatregoing transformed into a professional adult job, the shame about my South African identity being addressed through playing a South African part, and the sheer pleasure and privilege of interpreting great writing.

Fugard is one of the most original voices among contemporary playwrights. This partly comes, I think, from the fact that most of his characters would actually be talking in Afrikaans – certainly true of the poor whites in *Hello and Goodbye* – yet he writes them in English, while retaining some of the harsh rhythms and sharp sounds of Afrikaans, that veld language, that stone and thornbush tongue, which lends itself so well to the bare, primal stuff which is at the heart of his work. *Hello and Goodbye* is both a part of my life and one of my all-time great plays.

Characters (1989), *I.D.* (2003), *Year of the King* (2004), *Primo Time* (2005), *The Giant* (2007), *Beside Myself* (2009)

Ali Taylor

Theatre is shit. Or at least I thought so for most of my childhood. For me, theatre meant the annual panto at the Reading Hexagon. The Hexagon was a grim slab of '70s concrete in the town centre, and the pantos were a riot of pink and perms and teeth and filled with '80s light entertainers like Little and Large. It was something my family went to because a) it was free – a treat from my dad's company to its staff – and b) me and my sister got a toy at the end of the night. I can't remember much about the shows other than there were women dressed as boys (which was completely wrong) and they kept interrupting the story with singing (urghh). At that time, my interests were werewolves, vampires and Bryan Robson. And none of these ever featured.

At nine years old I wrote off theatre as naff and went back to making up my own stories with *Star Wars* figures and *M.A.S.K.*

I didn't have anything more to do with theatre until I was sixteen. It was work-experience time at school, and we had to choose where to go. The previous year I had worked in a garden centre, spending a week dead-heading pansies and collecting slugs in a bucket. Organising a slug genocide had been fun, but there was a chance to work at South Hill Park arts centre in Bracknell. For teenage me, Bracknell was properly glamorous. It had an Our Price and River Island – and in the '90s, the more rare Nirvana CDs and oatmeal T-shirts you had, the more kudos you got. So working at South Hill Park was a chance to avoid slugs, meet model-standard actresses (woo-hoo) and, most importantly, go shopping.

Arriving there I was told to go backstage. I was handed a cardboard cloud and told to scuttle up the rigging. Up there was an ASM called Becky, who said to be quiet and lower the cloud over the stage on her say-so. Peering down, I saw a group of young people preparing to sing. Singing! (Urghh.) Worthy community theatre! (Double urghh.) But – if you excuse me this shameless moment of cheese – the second that one of the girls started singing it was the most beautiful thing. Her voice was amazing. The audience was enthralled and went wild at the end. It was very special. I guess it must have flicked a switch. Theatre didn't have to mean naff or camp or Bobby fucking Davro. It could be honest and moving and communicate with people.

If the door to theatre had been edged open, it was at university in Warwick that I fell through it. By '96, I had ditched the oatmeal and curtains but had replaced them with pretensions to be a poet. To my eternal frustration I was a pretty bad poet but was fully in love with language and arrived on campus like a sponge ready to soak everything up. Through my course I was exposed to incredible manipulators of words like Pynchon, Morrison, Faulkner and Milton. And then there was the theatre module on contemporary writers like Pinter, Bond and Kane. These writers had that rare ability to elevate language into a style at once artificial but real, poetic but natural. I read and read and read.

Of course, I couldn't articulate why I was so taken with these playwrights at the time. I just knew I'd never heard anything like them and desperately wanted to copy them. I ditched the very bad poetry and began writing very bad plays.

By luck, three plays arrived on tour at Warwick Arts Centre that blew my head off. In my memory, they all came at once but they must have played over a year or two. But they are probably the key influences on everything I've written since.

The first was *Disco Pigs* by Enda Walsh, a play which used language like Kurt Cobain used a guitar. With the actors throwing themselves headlong into the story, it was like being hit by a wave of words and then pulled along on the rip tide. It was just thrilling.

At last I was watching a play aimed at people my age which felt modern and urgent and exciting.

Next up was *Blue Heart* by Caryl Churchill, two one-act plays which were very different in tone but which played with form and language. At the heart of both pieces was a theatricality that was inspiring.

And following that was a play far less radical, almost old-fashioned at a time of 'In Yer Face' but no less memorable. That was *The Weir* by Conor McPherson. I saw it on the same day Sarah Kane died and the director stepped onto the stage to tell everyone the terrible news. Whether that gave the show a greater resonance that night I don't know, but the ghost story gripped, and I can remember every turn of that beautifully wrought story even now fifteen years on.

If there are links between these plays it's that they are completely theatrical. They use the possibilities of theatre to enhance their storytelling.

And if there's one other thing they share it's real heart. The combination of theatricality and soul is still the touchstone for my writing and what I'm always aiming for.

Cotton Wool (2008), *Overspill* (2008), *The Machine Gunners* (2012, adapted from Robert Westall)

Polly Teale

The first play I can remember vividly was a production of Tennessee Williams's *The Glass Menagerie* at the Crucible in Sheffield, my home town, when I was about thirteen. I sat on the front row, so there was nothing between me and the actors, who seemed to burn in the darkness like the candles that Laura blows out at the end of the night. Hayley Mills played Laura, and I can still remember her excruciating shyness and the painful, exquisite pleasure of watching her transformed by the gentleman caller and hoping that somehow, miraculously, this might be the beginning of a new life for her. Of course, all hope comes crashing down as we discover that the gentleman caller is already betrothed and that Tom (who is Tennessee) must abandon his clinging mother and sister if he is to survive. Williams's brilliant play about the stifling claustrophobia of the family and the terrible burden of love and duty that binds us was completely enthralling. I remember, when it ended, having the thought that I wanted to follow them backstage and then, I think, the idea that somehow I might be part of that world. I had no idea how or that there was such a thing as a director or even a playwright, but walking back out onto the street it felt as though I was in exile – that I wanted to exist in a place where it was possible to express our most private fears and fantasies, our secret hopes and longings. To explore the relationship between the world we inhabit and our inner lives. To share our madness and understand that we are not alone.

Jane Eyre (1998, adapted from Charlotte Brontë), *After Mrs Rochester* (2003), *Brontë* (2005, 2011), *Mine* (2008), *Speechless* (2010, with Linda Brogan, adapted from Marjorie Wallace)

Steve Thompson

The first play I ever acted in was *The Wizard of Oz*. It was 1974 and I was seven years old. I was a Munchkin. I wore a bright green tunic, purple tights and a pixie hat. They gave me a flower cut out of hardboard to hide behind when Dorothy turned up. *'Come out, come out wherever you are and meet the young lady who fell from a star.'* You know the routine. The kid next to me on stage was called Tom. We crouched behind our flowers side by side – mine was red and his was yellow. For some reason – can't remember now – we got into an argument and had a fight. Blows were exchanged behind the big wooden petals. Tom was led offstage in floods of tears before the song was over. It was not only my first play, it was my first scrap. I was made to apologise in the green room by my mother. (She was dressed as the wicked witch, which made it all the more terrifying.)

The first play I had professionally produced was called *Damages*. It went on at the Bush in 2004. I was a house parent at the time – I'd quit teaching to stay home and look after my three children. My wife Lorna had bought me a laptop, and every night I sat on the landing, policing the kids at bedtime. I wrote *Damages* on that landing, whilst simultaneously barking 'Get back into bed' every five minutes. It was actually a play about Lorna. A friend of mine asked if she could read it. She gave it to someone who gave it to someone else who gave it to the Bush. In September 2003 I was standing in my kitchen. Lorna came downstairs and said, 'There's someone called Mike Bradwell on the phone.' I'd never met him but I knew who he was. My heart skipped a beat because I guessed why he was phoning. He said, 'I've read your play and I love it. Don't show it to anyone else.' It was the most thrilling moment. I'd never even thought about being a proper writer. It was directed by Roxana Silbert, who has directed most of my plays ever since, basically because she's terrific. The actors were Amanda Drew, John Bett, Phil McKee and Paul Albertson. All of them still have a special place in my heart because it was the first one. (I still see Paul. He's into organic health drinks. Keeps trying to make me drink the most appalling slop.)

Whipping It Up (2006), *Roaring Trade* (2009), *No Naughty Bits* (2011)

Jack Thorne

My First Play was called *The Wave* – it was an adaptation of the book by Morton Rhue (the pseudonym of Todd Strasser). I had arrived at university determined to either be a politician or an actor. I had discovered I wasn't very good at either, so thought I might try directing... Unfortunately, stage rights were too expensive for me – I think they were £45 a night at the time – so I decided to write a play of my own. I'd written a scene from *The Wave* for my GCSE coursework so I got that out, looked at it again and decided to write a full play.

It wasn't until after I wrote it that I considered I might also need to pay Todd Strasser for the rights to adapt his book – or at least get his permission – so I wrote to him. He wrote a lovely letter back asking for £250. I didn't have £250 so I never replied and did the play anyway.

And this is how I became a thief and all-round theatrical highwayman.

The play itself wasn't particularly brilliant, but because the story (his story, the book is amazing) was so good we did OK. And from the moment someone first laughed at one of my (weak) gags I knew I wanted to stay a writer.

Though I hadn't entirely given up on the acting and directing as it turned out... On the fourth night of our five-night run our Jewish lead took the Sabbath off as he told us he would and I stood in. If hearing other people laughing at other people saying my lines was good, hearing people laughing as I said them was even better. The next play I wrote – called *You Have Been Loved* (title stolen from a George Michael song – I know, I know, I was highly confused at the time) – I wrote, directed, starred in, got the girl, kissed the girl, and the piece ended with a five-minute monologue by me. That play worked less well.

But I'd got the bug. And twenty-two plays later, I got my first play professionally staged – *When You Cure Me* – at the Bush Theatre. And a publishing house called Nick Hern Books very kindly agreed to take me on.

When You Cure Me (2005), *Stacy & Fanny and Faggot* (2007), *2nd May 1997* (2009), *Bunny* (2010), *Mydidae* (2012)

Stephen Unwin

What was the first play I ever saw? I've no idea. What did I act in as a child? I don't know for certain. Did I see that play I think I saw when I was ten, or have I just imagined it? Speak, memory, as clearly as you can, but who knows whether or not you're telling the truth.

I have a vivid sensation of playing Joseph in a nativity play at primary school when I was six or seven. I remember wearing a prickly brown tunic – my mother must have made it – and, I think, a stuck-on cardboard beard. The Virgin Mary definitely wore blue, but I've no idea who she was – she's probably a merchant banker by now. I know I went to a fancy-dress party dressed as Adam, wearing just a fig leaf, because I've seen the photo, and I'm sure I played the part to perfection. I have an odd feeling that I saw Peter Brook's production of *A Midsummer Night's Dream* when I was ten – but maybe that's just because I've seen so many pictures of it – but I definitely saw the astonishingly beautiful Rupert Everett play Titania at our posh boarding school in the mid-1970s.

I saw a lot things at the Royal Court in my teens – mostly directed by Bill Gaskill – and I remember being (unsuccessfully) 'picked up' in the Royal Court Tavern by Desmond O'Donovan (an amazingly eccentric director and Catholic priest, who had been important at the Court in the 1960s), who gave me a 'backstage tour' and introduced me to the then Artistic Director, Stuart Burge, as 'the future of British theatre'! I told this story when I was interviewed to be Max Stafford-Clark's successor many years later: inexplicably, they gave the job to Stephen Daldry instead. Ha, bloody ha!

The first production I ever directed at school was Stoppard's *Albert's Bridge* (I must have been sixteen and enjoyed telling Tom this when I directed his *Rosencrantz and Guildenstern are Dead* twenty-five years later). The first play I directed at university was Wedekind's *Spring Awakening* (fifteen productions in three years: how did I find the time?). I remember knocking on Stephen Fry's door – a grandee of Cambridge drama, even in those days – to try to get the money. And I have a clear image in my first term of sitting in a pub listening to Simon (Russell, as he now is) Beale complain that as a 'big fat queen' he'd never play Hamlet, and Tilda Swinton announce that she was 'probably' more interested in film than theatre. *Où sont les neiges d'antan?*

I saw dozens of productions in my teens and early twenties which blew my mind (so many at Riverside Studios, interestingly, and mostly international): Joint Stock's *The Ragged Trousered Philanthropists,* Tadeusz Kantor's astounding *Wielopole Wielopole,* Peter Gill's *Measure for Measure,* Andrzej Wajda's *Crime and Punishment* and, above all, Ingmar Bergman's *Miss Julie,* which Pierre Audi (the founding father of the Almeida) dragged me off to, despite my ignorant protestations about 'the limitations of naturalism'…

My London debut was a student production of *Measure for Measure*, which I took to the 1981 Edinburgh Festival and went on to the Almeida in its opening season. The rain was dripping through the roof, and we ate pizzas in the ever-so-scruffy wine bar, which – like the rest of Upper Street – has changed out of all recognition. But we felt we were in at the beginning of something new, and we were right.

I suppose my proper first hit was *Man to Man* in 1987, a one-woman play with Tilda Swinton, first seen at the Traverse and then at the Royal Court. Ben Ormerod had lit the whole play with reflectors and we brought him coffee and chocolates to calm his nerves. I had to push Tilda on from the wings on the press night, she was so scared. I still have a picture of us standing outside the Court with our name up in lights. We look such kids.

I got lured into directing opera with the postwar premiere of Brecht/Eisler's *The Decision* at the Almeida Music Festival on election night 1987: the great and the good of the British left came (Eric Hobsbawm, Denis Healey and Margot Heinemann for God's sake!), but Mrs Thatcher still got re-elected. I launched English Touring Theatre in 1993 with Alan Cumming's *Hamlet*, which opened at the Crewe Lyceum (of all places!), toured the country and played the Donmar for a month. And my first show at the Rose was *A Christmas Carol*: the local authority funding came through on Christmas Eve and, in celebration, the cast sang a tearful encore of 'Silent Night'.

Then there were the flops, the 'also rans', the 'why the hell did I do that?' shows, and all the rest: many of them 'firsts', some of them best forgotten. But that's enough old soldier's tales for now – before I sink finally into my 'anecdotage'.

So You Want To Be A Theatre Director? (2004), *Ibsen's* A Doll's House: *Page to Stage* (2006), *La Ronde* (2007, with Peter Zombory-Moldovan, from Arthur Schnitzler), *The Complete Brecht Toolkit* (2013)

Harriet Walter

My First Play and all I can remember of it.

There was a man dressed as a dog called Nana, a girl dressed as a boy called Peter, and a man with long flouncy black hair and a girly hat called Captain Hook.

Then there was a lovely 'normal' ideal Mummy. Tall and soft-voiced and appropriately named Mrs Darling, and Daddy was a Darling too.

There were three children in long nighties and one had a top hat. They bounced and knelt on the top of the covers of their three beds in the night nursery and they shouted everything they had to say in ringing sing-song voices.

Nana the dog busied around the nursery with a man-on-all-fours lollop. Nana took a corner of a sheet in her mouth and drew it up around a reclining child and in that way tucked each one up in bed. Mrs Darling had to help Mr Darling do up his evening bow tie. Then Perfect Mother swished from bed to bed kissing her children goodnight before going out to some glamorous do and the children were left alone.

There was a window along the back wall and something flitted past it. A shiver and a shadow and then a tap-tap on the window pane. Some brave child opened the casement. The candles guttered and in flew Peter Pan.

I didn't particularly like him at first. He was a bit of a know-all and he whined about having lost his shadow which turned out to be a bit of lady's stocking stuck to his heel.

There was Tinkerbell who was just a juddering light that climbed walls and ceilings and had an irritating personality but something was building up inside me, an expectation, a challenge, a midnight feast. The danger of an adventure but the safety of following a leader. Suddenly I am hovering over the beds, flapping my arms, I am he and she and them and I am flying out of the open window into the dark, cushioned on pillows of hot night air.

* * *

Under the ground and in the caves between the roots of trees were the Lost Boys. They also shouted with sing-song voices but they were grubby and feral and they longed for a normal Mummy. They curled up at Wendy's feet lulled by her bedtime stories.

Meanwhile, in another part of the island, there was black-hatted, black-haired, moustachioed Captain Hook. He had a villain's bent back and roving searchlight eyes. When he whipped round to catch you out, the skirt tails of his coat flapped and swirled like black crows. He only had one fist to shake in threat. His other hand was made of iron and clawed at the air in fury.

The only thing that could frighten Captain Hook as much as he frightened me was the ticking croc. The crocodile had eaten Hook's hand and as far as I could understand that hand had turned into a clock inside the croc's tummy so that Captain Hook could hear him coming. I didn't see why the croc wanted revenge on Hook when Hook was the one who had had his hand eaten.

There was a pirate song which the pirates sang in bass notes that rumbled under the soles of my feet. The pirates stomped single file through the jungle. The ones I remembered were Starkey and Smee. Starkey wore a headscarf. He was Captain Hook's mate, or at least pretended to be. Smee was on my side. He was a bungler and frightened. He wore a striped shirt and sang a sad song outside his tent where he worked at a sewing machine. 'Poor Smee,' he intoned.

There was some routine whereby Smee was sent into a comic tizz by a loud ripping sound that made him twirl round and check out his trousers. I laughed and everybody in the audience laughed, and I was reminded that I wasn't in Neverland but was sitting amongst strangers in rows of dingy red velvet and gilt, wearing my best dress with a chocolate box on my knee.

There was a pirate ship and doomed men walked the plank. That was a literal phrase. They walked with hung heads along a plank and tipped into the devouring sea with a haunting howl and a splash. Doomed people could not fly away on a wire it seemed.

And Hook was doomed. The ticking clunking crocodile rounds a corner, yawns his snapping cardboard mask and tugs and tugs at Hook's good arm dragging him into the cavernous maw till the object of my terror is reduced to a pile of chewed black rags.

Tinkerbell bobs back into life having wilted in a papier-mâché corner of the set. We breathed her back into existence by believing in her.

The music imprints itself on my brain for years to come. I can still hum 'Yoho, Yoho, the pirate's song' and smell the dusty painty air of the theatre, and feel the shiny programme on my knee and remember blinking my eyes back to real matinee daylight on the Strand but not really being back in reality for quite a while.

Peter Pan became an annual fixture for a few years. The woman playing Peter sometimes changed, which felt like a betrayal until I was won over by Peter's defiant energy. Do you believe in fairies? You *must*! You *must* believe! Peter had a desperation, a need. Please allow me to stay as a child. Please allow me to be a boy. Please allow me to fly. If you believe, you allow me life.

Other People's Shoes: Thoughts on Acting (2003)

Steve Waters

You have to imagine a school: Long Lawford County Combined Primary School. It's outside Rugby and it's the mid-'70s. I am probably eight (records are thin on the ground). All I can recall is being in a community play, that embodiment of everything I still find beguiling about the 1970s; God knows who wrote it, but it was about (calm down) the history of Long Lawford. How an evening could be filled with such a nugatory history I leave to you to imagine – suffice to say the scene I was in was an early verbatim play based on parochial records, documenting a great historical injustice which I rather think David Hare was influenced by: the historic failure of Long Lawford to secure its own railway station. Perhaps something of the topical urgency of that piece remains in my work. I'd like to say from that day forth I acquired a passion for the stage, but I think even as an eight-year-old I had a sense this fodder was somewhat lacking in essential Aristotleian qualities.

Wait, back up. My actual first play probably even predated this. It had to be in Coventry, yes, it had to be in the Belgrade Theatre; it was surely a pantomime, where all the kids of employees at Rolls Royce Engineering were granted a free matinee. As we walk into the theatre we are foolishly given a box of chocolates and this becomes everything we remember about what follows. The comically bad panto is subordinated to us pelting the actors with soft-centred chocs and then, finally, resigned to the game, the actors returning fire. When Brecht wished for a sporting audience, detached and smoking a cigar, I don't think he had this level of disengagement in mind.

OK, moving forward; an anachronistic exam is passed and I find myself going to an anachronistic grammar school in Rugby (I have always lagged twenty or so years behind my times). Perhaps this would be the epiphanous moment when theatre would provide me with an escape route from a career in heavy industry. Certainly every year our librarian, Charlie Rankin, would hazard staging a play backed up by art teacher Mr Webb. In this instance I think it was *The King's Stag* by Goldoni; for God's sake, *The King's Stag*, in 1980, the nation tearing itself in two! What was Charlie Rankin thinking of? I believe (again records are thin on the ground) I played a courtier: there was certainly a mortifying periwig involved. I remember two things about this experience: firstly my parents and my sister sat on the front row of 'Big School', the venue, laughing themselves sick at me prancing around in my rococco outfit; and then, more shamefully, corpsing during a game of blind man's buff and in full view of the audience discharging an enormous quantity of snot into my cupped hands.

This experience might have been redeemed the following year in my performance as Simon Chachava in Brecht's *The Caucasian Chalk Circle*, but sadly, a week before the show, Big School burned to the ground. Arson was not suspected.

I'm struggling to find that epiphany. It wasn't the school trip to *Julius Caesar* at the RSC where I remember nothing but the actors' leather jackets; I don't think it was watching *Look Back in Anger* at the Warwick Arts Centre as that seemed to cement my lifelong loathing of that play (sorry Kenneth Tynan). None of these experiences come anywhere close to watching *2001: A Space Odyssey* at Rugby Theatre or being sneaked in to *Raging Bull* by my dad. But when I come to think of it, reading *The Duchess of Malfi* at sixth form, which coincided with Echo and the Bunnymen's album *Porcupine* with its track 'My White Devil' featuring the lyric: 'John Webster was one of the best there was / He was the author of two major tragedies' – this marked a definite change. Webster's savagery, density, the crazy mash-up of lycanthropy and incest, not to mention all that 'hunting badgers by owl-light' – this pierced me, woke me up in a way Shakespeare had failed to do. Getting an endorsement from Echo and the Bunnymen helped.

But I had still seen so little theatre, so few plays. Then my sister went to study Chemistry at Sheffield University; visiting her was a maelstrom of northern chic and sexy encounters with older women and yes, the Crucible Theatre, where we saw *A Passion in Seven Days* by Howard Barker, directed by Michael Boyd. (Wikipedia has just informed me it was in fact *A Passion in Six Days*, 1983; that told me.) A play about the Labour Party in freefall. In hectic Webster-like verse. In a socialist theatre in a socialist city. I remember almost nothing about it except those facts; it was as if I had entered into a room where the most intense conversation imaginable was happening, quite indifferent to me. It was a passionate, angry, sardonic place, a place of colour and vigour. Watching a play could be as exciting as watching a gig.

Yes, that was surely the one. I instantly forgot who wrote it. But when twenty years later Michael Grandage brought my *World Music* to the Crucible stage, the symbolism for me was particularly intense; certainly the brown carpet was still there; for me '70s furnishings, municipal socialism enacted in fixtures and fittings forever colours my sense of theatre.

Oh, and my first actual play as in the first play written by me?

I was a week into my first term reading English at Oxford. There was this thing called Cuppers, a competition. My motley fellow freshers wanted to perform something and, yes, I got dobbed in. It was called *Arthur Contrives a Settlement* (largely so it could create the acronym ACAS – remember them – something to do with trades unions and bargaining – remember that?). The whole thing was a confused skit on Scargill and the Miners' Strike (it was 1984); but tangled up with my struggle with learning Anglo-Saxon. To give you a sense of how bad it was, the dramatis personae included Offa the Dyke, The Venerable Bore and some-one called Cnut. Yet the judges (including Young Turks Katie Mitchell and Patrick Marber) saw some merit in it.

I dearly wish this had been a more inspiring account. I dearly wish I had written puppet plays for my family or gazed down on a latter-day Sarah Bernhardt sick with love. Theatre is after all about glamour, isn't it? But something must have happened when I put on my papier-mâché stovepipe hat and glued on my sideburns and enacted the epochal failure of Long Lawford to acquire its own railway station or else I wouldn't be writing this now, would I?

World Music (2003), *The Unthinkable* (2004), *Fast Labour* (2008), *The Contingency Plan* (2009), *The Secret Life of Plays* (2010), *Little Platoons* (2011), *Ignorance/Jahiliyyah* (2012)

Tom Wells

When I was seven my dad wrote a panto.

He was a pig farmer at the time but he's always written things too. Every so often at weddings, birthdays, church halls, barn dances, in pubs, folk clubs or old people's homes, any sort of a do, someone will ask if he's brought his guitar and, if he has, he'll nip and get it from the boot of the car. He usually explains before he starts, 'The idea of the singing's to drown out the guitar and the idea of the guitar's to drown out the singing', but the songs – 'The Ballad of the Peugeot Pick-up' (about trying to keep his knackered blue pick-up roadworthy), 'Half My Farm's in Holland Now' (about coastal erosion), or 'The Patrington Voluntary Fire Brigade' (about the Patrington Voluntary Fire Brigade) – always go down brilliantly. They're funny, sad and sometimes a bit romantic, in a gruff sort of way.

So it wasn't too odd for him to have written this panto. Still a surprise though.

He did it quickly on the back of brown envelopes, not in order, mostly in rhyming couplets. The first I knew about it was when various members of Derwent Young Farmers sat in a circle on our lounge floor one night and read it out. My Aunty Rack was the leading lady, Wicked Squire William played the electric guitar, and our cat Marigold sat in the middle licking her bum. It was another world.

Rehearsals moved to the village hall and me and my sister tagged along. One of the girls could do the splits so she was in charge of dance routines, and some stroppy but hilarious local twins were cast as fairies. My mum did costumes, which meant that a lot of our curtains turned up as villagers. She sort of found her calling in Birkie though, the dame. His dresses were stunning, made from the most exotic colours Flaxton jumble sale could manage, mixed with glittery ribbon and bits of neon net. And the boobs – the boobs were whopping, separate and had bells on the end. Birkie got very attached.

That was the first play I saw getting made. I'm lucky it was a good one. A bit scruffy, a bit rough round the edges, but full of heart and mischief. The best sort of play, I think.

Me, As a Penguin (2010), *The Kitchen Sink* (2011), *Jumpers for Goalposts* (2013)

Timothy West

The first play I remember seeing – I must have been about seven years old – was a Lancashire comedy by Ronald Gow entitled *Ma's Bit o'Brass*, performed in weekly rep at the Little Theatre, Bristol. My father, Lockwood West, was their leading man at the time, and I probably came most weeks to see him; but this is the play I remember, because he wore a droopy moustache, supped his tea from the saucer, and fell out of bed. I thought it was hilarious.

None of my schools (I went to thirteen: my parents moved about a lot) showed much interest in drama. There were no school plays, and visits to the theatre were restricted to viewing works that were on the school syllabus. Serious theatregoing for me didn't happen until I became a student at the polytechnic, Regent Street. Actually it wasn't all that serious: *The Chiltern Hundreds, Under the Sycamore Tree, The Happiest Days of Your Life…* I even took in a new piece called *The Mousetrap*.

Discovering one day there was life South of the Thames, I began to join the gallery queue at the Old Vic, and continued to do so for each play in Michael Benthall's five-year Shakespeare cycle. In that first year (1953) I saw Richard Burton as Hamlet, Coriolanus, Caliban, Sir Toby Belch and the Bastard in *King John*. The company also included Michael Hordern, Fay Compton, Claire Bloom, John Neville, Robert Hardy, William Squire and Paul Daneman. Crouching on my hard one-and-sixpenny bench, I was enthralled. Already an enthusiastic amateur actor, I was now harbouring secret thoughts about following my parents into the business (they weren't at all keen), and I used to think, gosh, if I could just *be* on that Old Vic stage, holding a spear, or even as a dead body... Little did I think that a generation later I'd be down there playing King Lear, Shylock, Falstaff – even *running* the place for a while.

My first actual performance on the professional stage came as a bit of a surprise. One Monday morning in February 1956 I started work as a student ASM at Wimbledon for the Peter Haddon Company, which presented weekly rep, unbelievably, in this 1,700-seat theatre. I had spent my first day sweeping the stage, going down to the station to collect the hired costumes and wigs for the dress rehearsal of Ugo Betti's *Summertime*, and making tea for the cast. And then as the rehearsal finished, Peter Haddon came up to me and said, 'We need a *farmer*, just at the end of the play. Just a couple of lines, nothing much.' He cast a quick eye over my threadbare jersey and grubby corduroys. 'You'll do as you are – but you'll need a hat. Ask Wardrobe.'

So that was My First Play as a performer; hardly a spectacular initiation into the world I had chosen to inhabit, but then I always was a slow developer, spending two more years as an acting ASM, in Newquay, Hull and Salisbury. What I learnt, though, being cast in the tiny parts of butlers, gardeners and police constables that went with my main stage-management duties, and finally going on to play proper parts as a fully fledged actor, was something I believe impossible for a young actor to achieve today. If you did forty-five plays in a year in a good company (or just twenty-two in the rarefied atmosphere of fortnightly rep), you might well at the end of that time have been introduced to Shakespeare, Sheridan, Congreve, Shaw, Wilde, Coward, Rattigan, O'Casey, Emlyn Williams and Agatha Christie, as well perhaps as Chekhov, Ibsen and Molière. Not just the styles of speech, but of dress, manners, personal sculpture, to say nothing of regional accents. You learnt the exciting trade of being versatile – a skill that sadly counts against you today, at least in film and television.

My first appearance in Shakespeare: *Macbeth*, at the Marlowe Theatre, Canterbury, as the Thane of Angus and a Murderer. Again, not an earth-shattering inauguration, but I did have that speech: 'The West yet glimmers with some streaks of day' – only two and a half lines, but wonderful.

Macbeth was directed by Clifford Williams, and five years later he offered me a part in David Rudkin's play, *Afore Night Come*, in the RSC's experimental season at the Arts Theatre. At that time I had done very little in the way of new work, and this play was a ground-breaking experience for most of us, audience and critics included. Going straight from that to Robert Bolt's *Gentle Jack*, a very smart West End production starring Edith Evans (and rather misunderstood by the H.M. Tennent management), gave me an insight into the contrasting ways in which new writers were being treated in the mid-'60s.

Meanwhile, the RSC decided to re-stage *Afore Night Come* as part of their 1964 season at the Aldwych. *Gentle Jack* meant I was not available to go with it, though ironically we came off just a week before the Rudkin play opened.

However, for some reason they were getting very fed up with the man who was playing my part, and, finding I was suddenly free, they re-employed me.

I therefore became part of the famed 'Dirty Plays' season at the Aldwych: *The Birthday Party, Endgame, The Jew of Malta,* Roger Vitrac's *Victor,* Henry Livings' *Eh?* and, of course, the *Marat/Sade.* In David Mercer's one-act *The Governor's Lady* I turned gradually from a Colonial grandee into a gorilla, and raped the distinguished Patience Collier under a mosquito net.

I suppose I could be said to have arrived.

I'm Here I Think, Where Are You? (1994), *A Moment Towards the End of the Play* (2002, 2010), *So You Want To Be An Actor?* (2005, with Prunella Scales)

Amanda Whittington

Nottingham, 1984. I'm fifteen years old. How I first come across her, I don't quite recall. We perhaps read an extract at school? Did I borrow the book from my teacher or go to the library? I know plays weren't easy to find.

The title's a promise, the name of the writer a poem. I turn the page and I read.

All the playwrights I've heard of are old, dead or male. She's nineteen – or she was when she wrote it – from Salford and wildly alive. She writes about working-class women, in words that are witty and painful, truthful and raw, yet sparkle and shimmer and sing.

Scenes written a decade before I was born feel fresh as a number-one single. I instinctively know she's a radical voice. Later, I'll learn how 'the personal is political', but, now, I just sense it is.

A teenage girl talking of class, gender, sexuality and race. Talking of life in all its complexity. Jo and Helen leapt off the page and into my consciousness. There they remain to this day, and they're echoed in each play I write.

The first copy I had fell apart long ago. I now have a second-hand reprint, with '£2.50' scribbled inside and the front page ripped out, who knows why? And this is just as it should be: a ragged, romantic, imperfect, rough diamond that lives in the room where I write.

A Taste of Honey – Shelagh Delaney. Six words that still sound like a record and read like a spell. The first play that spoke in my language and whispered: 'I did this, so maybe you can?' She is the greatest of writers, and thirty years after I read her, that promise holds true. By finding her voice, I found mine.

Be My Baby (2000), *Satin 'n' Steel* (2005), *Ladies' Day* (2006), *Ladies Down Under* (2007), *The Thrill of Love* (2013)

Nicholas Wright

The auditions were being held in a converted Dutch Reformed Church hall in the main street of Cape Town. Two women were organising things, one small and excitable, clanging with exotic beads and bangles, the other one gruff in corduroy slacks and brogues. This was my first sight of Gwen Ffrangcon-Davies and Marda Vanne, who would play the roles of the governess and the housekeeper in *The Innocents*, a play based on Henry James's *The Turn of the Screw*, in which two children are thought to have been corrupted by ghosts.

I was handed a couple of pages. The part I was auditioning for was that of a boy of twelve, my age, who had been mysteriously expelled from school and was being quizzed about this by his governess. I had been acting on the radio since I was six years old, so sight-reading was a pushover and I carried the scene off pretty well. Gwen and Marda exchanged a meaningful look, and I was given the playscript. 'Let's read a bit more,' said Gwen.

I began to read, gathering the situation as I went along. 'Weren't your brothers ever naughty… in a *grown-up* way?' I asked, ladling on the dark insinuation that the line suggested. 'I don't know,' Gwen replied with heart-stirring pathos, though it was nothing compared to the pathos I produced on my next line. 'I… I wish I could go away.' ('His voice dying away,' it said in the script.) The scene warmed up. Had I stolen things at school, Gwen asked. Was that why I had been expelled? It seemed that whatever I'd done was worse than that. Cornered, I lashed out. 'You're dirty, dirty, dirty,' I hissed. Gwen's eyes lit up with the gleam of competition. 'You've never stopped seeing him, have you Miles?' she cried, 'him' being the valet who had corrupted me. 'You still want to be with him, don't you?' My big moment had arrived. 'He's dead!' I uttered in a deafening scream. All that was left was for me to turn to the French windows, banish the ghost for ever and crash lifeless but triumphantly to the floor.

A few weeks later I and the little girl who was to play my sister were staying in a farmhouse a short walk across the veld to the house where these two very unusual women were living, and where we would be rehearsing. Gwen, as I would call her when I was older, had been a great star of the London theatre. She was a marvellous actress, as romantic in her style as you might expect from one old enough to have known Ellen Terry, but at the same time capable of great primitive power. Marda, whom I would also get to know and love, was South African. As a young woman she had been wooed by an up-and-coming Transvaal lawyer, and in exasperation had agreed to marry him for a year, a promise she followed up to the letter, slamming the door on him twelve months to the day after the wedding. Fortunately or not, he got over the shock, went into politics and became Prime Minister: J.G. Strijdom, the architect of apartheid. Marda and Gwen met in London in the 1920s, and, when war broke out, Marda, who was in some ways rather a cowardly lion (she used to hide under the table at the sound of thunder), persuaded Gwen to come with her to South Africa, much to the detriment of Gwen's career.

On our first day of rehearsal, Gwen explained what she wanted from me. I was not to be phoney, she said. 'A lot of actors are phoney, even very famous ones, but if *you* are phoney, I shall stop you and you will have to do it over and over again.'

When we put down the books, things got tricky. 'Why are you standing like a girl?' she asked, staring at my legs. 'I don't know,' I said. She wouldn't give up. 'Do you stand like that when you're doing a play at school?' 'I suppose I do,' I replied. 'What was the last part you played?' 'Alice in Wonderland,' I mumbled miserably. 'That explains it, Doodley,' Marda barked, taking her cigar out of her mouth. 'Never mind, Doodles,' Gwen replied. 'We'll just have to teach him to stand properly.'

Thus, over innumerable painful, tearful sessions I learned some basic rules of acting. Stand firmly on both feet. Keep your arms relaxed and don't wave your hands about or jiggle your head. Breathe deeply, speak up, say every line as though it had just come into your head that very minute and, above all, be *real*.

Our first night was tense. 'Doodley, look at our leading man!' Marda cried, grouchy in her hated pinny and mobcap. 'Just *look* at him! He's only *a little boy!*' But my performance caused a sensation, partly because people started writing to the newspapers saying that acting in the play was causing my moral and physical ruin. I had developed the Donald Wolfit trick of panting in supposed exhaustion at the curtain-call, which made the scandal worse. In order to calm it down, I had to be photographed all round Cape Town doing normal boy-like things like kicking a rugby ball and sliding down banisters. It was a relief to get back to the theatre, where I could put on my mascara and scream at ghosts.

Late in the run, Gwen received an offer from Tyrone Guthrie to play Queen Katherine in his all-star coronation production of *Henry VIII* at the Old Vic. 'It's Paul Rogers, Leo Genn and Alexander Knox,' she said crossly. 'I don't call *that* an all-star cast!' But she went back to London: after many years in the wilderness, this was a big break for her. Six years later, when I arrived in England to go to drama school, both she and Marda were unutterably kind to me. By then, I had lost whatever acting talent I'd possessed as a child. What I had left was the love of theatre that they had taught me. It took me years to find a way of using it.

Mrs Klein (1988, 2009), *John Gabriel Borkman* (1996, from Ibsen), *Naked* (1998, from Pirandello), *Cressida* (2000), *Wright: Five Plays* (2000), *Lulu* (2001, from Wedekind), *Vincent in Brixton* (2002), *Three Sisters* (2003, from Chekhov), *His Dark Materials* (2003, 2004, adapted from Philip Pullman), *Thérèse Raquin* (2006, adapted from Zola), *The Reporter* (2007), *Rattigan's Nijinsky* (2011, adapted from Terence Rattigan), *The Last of the Duchess* (2011, adapted from Caroline Blackwood), *Travelling Light* (2012)

Nick Hern Books 1988–2013
A Chronology of Firsts

1988

Nick Hern Books first comes into being under the auspices of Walker Books.

Mrs Klein by Nicholas Wright is NHB's first play and is the first NHB play to transfer to the West End and Broadway.

1989

Cloud Nine is the first of Caryl Churchill's plays published by NHB.

A collection of short plays by David Edgar, *Edgar: Shorts*, is the first time Edgar is published by NHB.

Max Stafford-Clark's first book, *Letters to George*, is published.

A Handful of Stars, the first of Billy Roche's plays, is published.

Diving for Pearls, a novel, is the first title by Howard Brenton published by NHB.

An Enemy of the People adapted from Ibsen is the first of two titles by Arthur Miller published by NHB.

A double volume of *Smelling a Rat* and *Ecstasy* marks the first appearance of Mike Leigh on the NHB list.

H.I.D. is the first play by Howard Brenton published by NHB.

Ghetto by Joshua Sobol in an adaptation by David Lan is the first NHB play to win the Evening Standard Best Play Award.

Driving Miss Daisy by Alfred Uhry is the first of hundreds of titles published by Theatre Communications Group in the USA to be distributed by NHB.

Characters is the first book by Antony Sher published by NHB.

1990

Valued Friends is the first of Stephen Jeffreys' plays published by NHB.

Shooting the Actor is the first book by Simon Callow published by NHB.

Sunday in the Park with George is the first title by Stephen Sondheim published by NHB, and the first Pulitzer Prize-winner on the NHB list.

Profiles is the first title by Kenneth Tynan published by NHB.

Scot-Free sees the first publication by NHB of a number of Scottish playwrights including John/Jo Clifford (*Losing Venice*); Rona Munro (*Saturday at the Commodore*); Chris Hannan (*Elizabeth Gordon Quinn*).

A double volume of *My Heart's a Suitcase* and *Low Level Panic* contains the first of Clare McIntyre's plays published by NHB.

1991

Death and the Maiden is the first of Ariel Dorfman's plays published by NHB and the first NHB play to win an Olivier Award for Play of the Year (in 1992).

Long Day's Journey into Night is the first of ten volumes of Eugene O'Neill's plays published by NHB.

Rona Munro's Evening Standard Most Promising Playwright Award for *Bold Girls* marks the first time NHB writers win the Award three years running (Stephen Jeffreys in 1989; Clare McIntyre in 1990).

1992

Angels in America is the first of Tony Kushner's plays published by NHB and the first NHB play to win a Tony Award (in 1993).

1993

Nick Hern Books becomes an independent limited company for the first time, based in Nick Hern's back bedroom. The first book published by Nick Hern Books Limited is Michael Billington's *One Night Stands*.

The Normal Heart is the first of two plays by Larry Kramer published by NHB.

Laban for Actors and Dancers, the first of two books on Laban by Jean Newlove, is published.

1994

Nick Hern Books wins its first award: 'Sunday Times Small Publisher of the Year'.

I'm Here I Think, Where Are You?, the first of two autobiographical books by Timothy West, is published.

NHB publishes the first six titles in its Drama Classics series (nearly 100 titles strong by 2013).

The Winslow Boy, the first volume in a definitive edition of Terence Rattigan, is published.

Anna Karenina is the first of Helen Edmundson's plays and adaptations published by NHB.

My Night With Reg is the first of Kevin Elyot's plays published by NHB.

The Hamster Wheel is the first play by Marie Jones published by NHB (her second, in 2000, is *Stones in His Pockets*).

1995

Jez Butterworth's first play, *Mojo*, is published.

Kindertransport is the first of Diane Samuels' plays published by NHB.

1996

This Lime Tree Bower is the first title by Conor McPherson published by NHB (the second is *St Nicholas* in 1997; in the same volume is an unperformed, unknown play called *The Weir*).

Hamlet: A User's Guide, the first book by Michael Pennington is published (though *The English Shakespeare Company* co-authored by Pennington and Michael Bogdanov was published in 1990).

The Shawshank Redemption is the first in NHB's series of Shooting Scripts.

1997

Disco Pigs is the first of Enda Walsh's plays published by NHB.

Ayub Khan-Din's first play, *East is East*, is published.

Peggy, the authorised biography of Peggy Ramsay by Colin Chambers, wins the first Theatre Book Prize.

1998

NHB moves into its first proper offices.

House of Games, the first book by Chris Johnston, is published.

Jane Eyre is the first of Polly Teale's plays and adaptations published by NHB.

The Honest Whore by Thomas Dekker is the first in NHB's series of Globe Quartos.

Quelques Fleurs is the first of Liz Lochhead's plays and adaptations published by NHB.

Arabian Nights is the first of Dominic Cooke's plays and adaptations published by NHB.

One Good Beating is the first of Linda McLean's plays published by NHB.

Bad Weather is the first of Robert Holman's plays published by NHB. (His novel, *The Amish Landscape*, had been published in 1992.)

1999

Howie the Rookie, the first of Mark O'Rowe's plays, is published.

Evoking Shakespeare is the first book by Peter Brook published by NHB.

2000

Be My Baby is the first of Amanda Whittington's plays published by NHB.

The first publication of Peter Nichols's *Diaries* is one of three titles by Nichols published this year.

The Pulitzer Prize-winning *Wit* is the first play by Margaret Edson published by NHB.

2001

Hamlet is the first title in NHB's Shakespeare Folios series.

Midden, the first play by Morna Regan, is published.

2002

The Actor and the Target, Declan Donnellan's first book, is published. It is the first NHB title published in Chinese – as well as in French, German, Spanish, Danish, Czech, Italian and Polish.

Finding Your Voice by Barbara Houseman, the first of several voice books from NHB, is published.

2003

Playing Lear is published, the first of two books by Oliver Ford Davies.

Duck, the first of Stella Feehily's plays, is published.

Protection, the first of Fin Kennedy's plays, is published.

Peribanez, the first of Tanya Ronder's plays and adaptations, is published by NHB.

Other People's Shoes marks Harriet Walters' first appearance on the NHB list.

World Music is the first of Steve Waters' plays published by NHB.

2004

Honour is the first of Joanna Murray-Smith's plays published by NHB.

dirty butterfly, the first of debbie tucker green's plays, is published.

So You Want To Be A Theatre Director? by Stephen Unwin is the first in NHB's *So You Want…* series.

Actions by Marina Caldarone and Maggie Lloyd-Williams is the first book on Actioning published by NHB. It becomes the first NHB book to sell more than 20,000 copies in the UK.

The Pull of Negative Gravity is the first play by Jonathan Lichtenstein published by NHB.

How Love is Spelt is published, the first of Chloë Moss's plays.

Brazil is the first play by Ronan O'Donnell published by NHB.

2005

Don Carlos is the first of Mike Poulton's plays and adaptations published by NHB.

Cruising, the first of Alecky Blythe's plays, is published.

One Day All This Will Come to Nothing, the first of Catherine Grosvenor's plays and adaptations, is published.

The Sugar Wife, the first play by Elizabeth Kuti, is published.

When You Cure Me is the first of Jack Thorne's plays published by NHB.

So You Want To Be An Actor? marks the first appearance on the NHB list of Prunella Scales, writing in consort with Timothy West.

2006

Food, co-written with Christopher Heimann, is the first play by Joel Horwood published by NHB.

Rabbit, the first of Nina Raine's plays, is published.

Steve Thompson's first play, *Whipping It Up*, is published.

Why Is That So Funny?, the first book by John Wright, is published.

2007

The first edition of NHB's *Guide to Plays for Performance* is sent out to amateur and student drama groups.

Bella Merlin's *The Complete Stanislavsky Toolkit* is the first of NHB's Toolkits (the second, on Brecht by Stephen Unwin, follows in 2013).

Different Every Night, Mike Alfreds' first book, is published.

The Enchantment, the first of Clare Bayley's plays and adaptations, is published.

The first winner of the first Bruntwood Prize for Playwriting, *Pretend You Have Big Buildings* by Ben Musgrave, is published by NHB.

The Pain and the Itch is the first of Bruce Norris's plays published by NHB.

Free Outgoing by Anupama Chandrasekhar is the first play from India published by NHB.

2008

August: Osage County is the first play by Tracy Letts published by NHB.

The Pride, the first of Alexi Kaye Campbell's plays, is published.

Tinderbox, the first of Lucy Kirkwood's plays, is published.

Cotton Wool, the first play by Ali Taylor, is published.

Cockroach is the first play by Sam Holcroft published by NHB.

2009

The first volume of NHB's Drama Games series is published: *Drama Games for Classrooms and Workshops* by Jessica Swale.

Jez Butterworth's *Jerusalem* is published, the first NHB play to transfer from the Royal Court Theatre to the West End to Broadway and back to the West End.

Eight, the first of Ella Hickson's plays, is published.

Little Gem, Elaine Murphy's first play, is published.

Talking Theatre is the first book by Richard Eyre published by NHB (though his adaptation of *Hedda Gabler* was published in 2005).

When the Rain Stops Falling is the first play by Andrew Bovell published by NHB.

2010

Bruce Norris's *Clybourne Park* is the first NHB play to win all four major drama awards on either side of the Atlantic: Olivier, Evening Standard, Tony and Pulitzer.

Me, As a Penguin, the first of Tom Wells's plays, is published.

Breed is the first play by Lou Ramsden published by NHB.

The Reluctant Escapologist marks Mike Bradwell's first appearance on the NHB list, and wins the Theatre Book Prize.

2011

Vivienne Franzmann's Bruntwood Prize-winning first play, *Mogadishu*, is published.

London Road by Alecky Blythe and Adam Cork is the first 'verbatim musical' published by NHB.

No Romance, the first of Nancy Harris's plays, is published.

Moment is the first of Deirdre Kinahan's plays published by NHB.

Foxfinder is the first play by Dawn King published by NHB.

Perve is the first play by Stacey Gregg published by NHB.

2012

Shakespeare's Lost Play is the first book by Gregory Doran published by NHB (though his reconstruction of *Cardenio* had been published in 2011).

NHB publishes its first ebooks: Jez Butterworth's *Jerusalem* and Simon Callow's *My Life in Pieces.*

Mark Rylance's first play, *I Am Shakespeare*, is published.

The Golden Rules of Acting marks Andy Nyman's first appearance on the NHB list.

World Scenography edited by Peter McKinnon and Eric Fielding is the first of three planned volumes covering stage design throughout the world.

So You Want To Be In Musicals? marks the first appearance of Ruthie Henshall (writing with Daniel Bowling) on the NHB list.

2013

NHB releases its first app, based on *Actions* by Marina Caldarone and Maggie Lloyd-Williams.

Bull is the first play by Mike Bartlett published by NHB (though NHB has been handling the amateur performing rights to all his earlier plays).

Speaking the Speech is the first book by Giles Block published by NHB.

NHB celebrates its first twenty-five years of publishing.

www.nickhernbooks.co.uk

 facebook.com/nickhernbooks

 twitter.com/nickhernbooks